MARIJUANA

MARIJUANA

Other books in the At Issue series:

MARIJUANA

Mary E. Williams, *Book Editor*

Daniel Leone, *President*
Bonnie Szumski, *Publisher*
Scott Barbour, *Managing Editor*
Helen Cothran, *Senior Editor*

San Diego • Detroit • New York • San Francisco • Cleveland
New Haven, Conn. • Waterville, Maine • London • Munich

LIBRARY OF CONGRESS CATALOGING-IN-PUBLICATION DATA

Marijuana / Mary E. Williams, book editor.
   p. cm. — (At issue)
Includes bibliographical references and index.
ISBN 0-7377-1572-3 (pbk. : alk. paper) — ISBN 0-7377-1571-5 (lib. : alk. paper)
   1. Marijuana. 2. Marijuana—Therapeutic use. 3. Marijuana—Law and legislation—United States. I. Williams, Mary E., 1960– . II. At issue (San Diego, Calif.)
HV5822.M3 M2673 2003
362.29'5—dc21   2002035386

Printed in the United States of America

Contents

Introduction

Marijuana is a psychoactive drug made from the dried leaves and flowers of the hemp plant *(cannabis sativa)*. Currently, the U.S. federal government classifies marijuana as a Schedule I substance—identifying it as having "a high potential for abuse" and "no currently accepted medical use," and placing it in the same league as opium and LSD. Because of its Schedule I status, it is illegal to buy, sell, grow, or possess marijuana in the United States, and people convicted of marijuana offenses face penalties ranging from fines to life imprisonment. In addition, the federal government, state governments, and local communities spend hundreds of millions of dollars annually on preventative programs such as Drug Abuse Resistance Education (DARE), in which police officers visit schools to teach young people to refrain from trying marijuana and other drugs.

Cannibis sativa has not always been classified as a dangerous narcotic. As early as the 1600s, colonists in Virginia and Massachusetts cultivated cannabis to produce hemp fiber, which was useful for creating strong cloth and twine. In the 1700s, the British parliament paid bounties for hemp and distributed manuals on hemp cultivation to dissuade American colonists from relying only on tobacco as a cash crop. By the 1840s, the therapeutic potential of cannabis extracts gained a modicum of recognition among U.S. physicians, and starting in 1850, the drug was included in the *U.S. Pharmacopoeia* as a recognized medicine. Solutions and tinctures containing cannabis were frequently prescribed for relieving pain and inducing sleep.

By the turn of the twentieth century, new drugs such as aspirin began to replace cannabis as a pain reducer, and marijuana, in its smokable form, gained notoriety as an intoxicant. During this time, recreational use of the drug occurred primarily among poor minorities and immigrants, particularly Mexican American migrants, Filipino laborers, southern blacks, and black jazz musicians. The general public's opinion of marijuana began to shift in the 1920s as use of the drug appeared to be correlated with a rising crime rate. Some politicians and civic leaders, reflecting the anti-immigrant sentiments of the time, claimed that marijuana abuse among ethnic minorities was largely the cause of increased crime and violence. Several state and local governments began a vigorous campaign against marijuana and its primary users. A 1917 editorial in a San Antonio, Texas, newspaper reported that "the hemp plant is a dangerous narcotic from which dangerous vice is acquired among the lower classes in Mexico. The men who smoke this herb become excited to such an extent that they go through periods of near frenzy." Similarly, in 1934, Harry Anslinger, the head of the Federal Bureau of Narcotics, stated that "fifty percent of the violent crimes committed in the districts occupied by Mexicans, Filipinos, Greeks, Spaniards, Latin-Americans, and Negroes may be traced to abuse of marijuana." Some contemporary analysts contend that marijuana received the blame for social ills that were actually rooted in the deeper national problems of poverty and racial prejudice.

Marijuana was not the only substance targeted by anti-drug activists during the early twentieth century. In the 1920s, Congress banned the use of alcohol and hard drugs and considered the prohibition of medicinal pain killers and caffeine. Yet after the ban on alcohol was lifted, the campaign against marijuana continued. In an effort to prevent marijuana abuse, political and law enforcement leaders often made exaggerated claims about the drug's effects. A notorious example of such exaggeration is seen in the 1936 educational film *Reefer Madness*, in which marijuana is depicted as causing vivid hallucinations, insanity, murder, and suicide. By this time, most states had laws prohibiting either the use, sale, or possession of marijuana. Then, in 1937, Congress passed the Marijuana Tax Act, which, rather than outlawing the substance, imposed a high tax on its growers, sellers, and buyers. As a result of this act, all medical products containing cannabis were withdrawn from the market, and in 1941, the drug was dropped from recognition by the *U.S. Pharmacopoeia*.

During the 1960s, marijuana became the most popular recreational drug among segments of the countercultural movement—a group composed largely of young adults and left-wing activists who demanded free speech on college campuses, opposed the war in Vietnam, and challenged mainstream cultural values. Subsequently, many of those who wished to protect the status quo came to see marijuana as a threat to the moral fiber of the nation. At the same time, the public became increasingly concerned about the rising rates of abuse of heroin, amphetamines, and LSD. In response to these concerns, Congress passed the Controlled Substances Act of 1970 (CSA), which established a new classification system for drugs based on their potential for abuse. Existing state laws that regulated illicit drugs, though they remained in effect, were overridden by the new federal statute. Under this law, all drugs considered to have a high potential for abuse and no generally accepted medical use would be defined as Schedule I drugs. Hence, marijuana was placed in Schedule I of the CSA.

Throughout the 1970s, however, public opinion about marijuana was mixed. A growing number of people were smoking marijuana to cope with medical problems that were not responsive to conventional medicine—particularly the pain and nausea associated with cancer and chemotherapy. Moderate politicians in both political parties began to argue in favor of marijuana decriminalization, which would waive serious penalties for possession of small amounts of marijuana for personal use. By the late 1970s, the American Medical Association, the American Bar Association, and the National Council of Churches all endorsed decriminalization, and eleven states had passed statutes that decriminalized marijuana use. But during the 1980 presidential campaign, Ronald Reagan took a hard line against marijuana, arguing that it was "probably the most dangerous drug in America today." According to journalist Eric Schlosser, the national War on Drugs, which began in 1982 under the Reagan administration, began as a war on marijuana: "[Reagan's] first drug czar, Carlton Turner, blamed marijuana for young people's involvement in 'anti-big-business, anti-authority demonstrations.' Turner also thought that smoking pot could transform young men into homosexuals."

Many current supporters of marijuana's Schedule I status grant that the twentieth century's anti-marijuana campaigns too often resorted to misinformation and bigotry, which ultimately proved to be counterproductive. Yet they also cite a growing body of scientific evidence that documents the health risks associated with marijuana use—risks which they believe warrant the continued criminalization of the drug. According to the National Institute on Drug Abuse (NIDA), acute marijuana intoxication induces euphoria accompanied by confusion, distorted perception, and coordination problems; high doses can cause delusions and paranoia. Short-term health effects of the drug include memory loss, anxiety, an increased heart rate, and decreased cognitive skills; long-term consequences for chronic smokers include a weakened immune system and an increased risk of cancer, respiratory diseases, and heart problems. In addition, marijuana opponents argue that many users become psychologically dependent on the "high" the drug creates. Such dependence can result in stunted emotional and social maturity as these users lose interest in school, work, and social activities.

Marijuana is also viewed by some analysts as a "gateway" drug that can lead to the abuse of other dangerous and illegal substances, including cocaine and heroin. According to Joseph Califano, chair of the National Center of Addiction and Substance Abuse, "Twelve-to-seventeen-year-olds who smoke marijuana are eighty-five times more likely to use cocaine than those who do not. Among teens who report no other problem behaviors, those who used cigarettes, alcohol, and marijuana at least once in the past month are almost seventeen times likelier to use . . . cocaine, heroin, or LSD." Califano notes that while most youths who smoke marijuana may not move on to harder drugs, the fact that a certain percentage of smokers will try heroin or cocaine suggests that the best strategy in preventing drug abuse is to maintain strong social sanctions against marijuana.

Critics of U.S. marijuana policy, on the other hand, argue that most anti-drug campaigners continue to exaggerate the dangers of marijuana. They contend that the majority of marijuana users suffer no lasting harm, do not move on to other drugs, and do not become addicts. While they grant that adolescents should not be permitted to smoke marijuana, they often maintain that the responsible use of the drug by adults for either recreational or medicinal purposes should not be illegal. Legalization proponents admit that any drug can be abused, and that no drug is entirely harmless or free of long-term health effects, but they believe that marijuana's mild intoxicating effects make it no more dangerous to society than alcohol or nicotine. In fact, states R. Keith Stroup, founder of the National Organization for the Reformation of Marijuana Laws (NORML), alcohol and tobacco "are the most commonly used and abused drugs in America and unquestionably they cause far more harm to the user and to society than does marijuana." In Stroup's opinion, "Congress needs to . . . stop legislating as if marijuana smokers were dangerous people who need to be locked up. Marijuana smokers are simply average Americans. . . . Whether one smokes marijuana or drinks alcohol to relax is simply not an appropriate area of concern for the government."

In recent years, a growing number of commentators of various political persuasions have questioned why it is legal for adults to become intoxicated with alcohol but not with marijuana. Some see this inconsistency as an unacknowledged hypocrisy rooted in historical cultural bias. In the United States, they argue, alcohol has long been the recreational drug of choice of America's dominant cultural group, and campaigns to prohibit it were unsuccessful. Marijuana use, which first emerged among non-white immigrants and minorities and later reappeared as the preferred drug of the 1960s counterculture, became an easy target for criminalization by powerful elites who harbored various prejudices. As *National Review* editor Richard Lowry explains, "Marijuana prohibition basically relies on cultural prejudice. . . . Many of [the drug's] advocates over the years have looked and thought like [countercultural icon] Allen Ginsberg. But that isn't much of an argument for keeping it illegal, and if marijuana started out culturally alien, it certainly isn't anymore."

But others discount the cultural prejudice theory as the explanation for the continued prohibition of marijuana. Some argue that the marijuana high is significantly different than the intoxication of alcohol. As journalist Damon Linker maintains, "While alcohol primarily diminishes one's inhibitions and clarity of thought, marijuana inspires a euphoria that resembles nothing so much as the pleasure that normally arises only in response to the accomplishment of the noblest human deeds," allowing its users "a means to enjoy the rewards of excellence without possessing it themselves." Such "unearned" euphoria is dangerous for both youths and adults, Linker contends, because it can destroy one's ambition to pursue the kinds of activity that would bring about normal pleasure. Ultimately, he concludes, marijuana use results in a "pathology of the soul" that would be most harmful to the developing minds of youths—who would have easier access to the drug if it were legalized for adults.

Whether marijuana's potential harms outweigh its benefits remains a central question in current debates about this controversial drug. The authors in *At Issue: Marijuana* present various opinions on the effects of marijuana and discuss some of the public policy measures concerning its status as a Schedule I drug.

1

Marijuana Is Harmful

Drug Enforcement Administration

The Drug Enforcement Administration (DEA) is the federal agency charged with enforcing the nation's drug laws.

Marijuana is a harmful and addictive drug. The short-term effects of marijuana use include memory loss, anxiety, and a decrease in cognitive and motor skills; long-term consequences include a weakened immune system and an increased risk of cancer, respiratory diseases, and heart problems. Marijuana smokers are also more likely to take other illegal drugs such as cocaine and heroin than are non-marijuana users. Smokable marijuana is not recommended for medical purposes as it can further compromise the health of those suffering from cancer, AIDS, and other chronic ailments. The attempt to legalize medical marijuana is actually part of a larger effort to legalize all drugs.

Does marijuana pose health risks to users?
• Marijuana is an addictive drug with significant health consequences to its users and others. Many harmful short-term and long-term problems have been documented with its use.

• The short-term effects of marijuana use include: memory loss, distorted perception, trouble with thinking and problem solving, loss of motor skills, decrease in muscle strength, increased heart rate, and anxiety.

• In recent years there has been a dramatic increase in the number of emergency room mentions of marijuana use. From 1993–2000, the number of emergency room marijuana mentions more than tripled.

• There are also many long-term health consequences of marijuana use. According to the National Institutes of Health, studies show that someone who smokes five joints per week may be taking in as many cancer-causing chemicals as someone who smokes a full pack of cigarettes every day.

• Marijuana contains more than 400 chemicals, including most of the harmful substances found in tobacco smoke. Smoking one marijuana cigarette deposits about four times more tar into the lungs than a filtered tobacco cigarette.

• Harvard University researchers report that the risk of a heart attack

Drug Enforcement Administration, "Marijuana: The Facts," www.usdoj.gov, 2001.

is five times higher than usual in the hour after smoking marijuana.

• Smoking marijuana also weakens the immune system and raises the risk of lung infections. A Columbia University study found that a control group smoking a single marijuana cigarette every other day for a year had a white-blood-cell count that was 39 percent lower than normal, thus damaging the immune system and making the user far more susceptible to infection and sickness.

• Users can become dependent on marijuana to the point they must seek treatment to stop abusing it. In 1999, more than 200,000 Americans entered substance abuse treatment primarily for marijuana abuse and dependence.

Marijuana is an addictive drug with significant health consequences to its users and others.

• More teens are in treatment for marijuana use than for any other drug or for alcohol. Adolescent admissions to substance abuse facilities for marijuana grew from 43 percent of all adolescent admissions in 1994 to 60 percent in 1999.

• Marijuana is much stronger now than it was decades ago. According to data from the Potency Monitoring Project at the University of Mississippi, the tetrahydrocannabinol (THC) content of commercial-grade marijuana rose from an average of 3.71 percent in 1985 to an average of 5.57 percent in 1998. The average THC content of U.S.-produced sinsemilla increased from 3.2 percent in 1977 to 12.8 percent in 1997.

Marijuana as medicine

Does marijuana have any medical value?

• Any determination of a drug's valid medical use must be based on the best available science undertaken by medical professionals. The Institute of Medicine conducted a comprehensive study in 1999 to assess the potential health benefits of marijuana and its constituent cannabinoids. The study concluded that smoking marijuana is not recommended for the treatment of *any* disease condition. In addition, there are more effective medications currently available. *For those reasons, the Institute of Medicine concluded that there is little future in smoked marijuana as a medically approved medication.*

• Advocates have promoted the use of marijuana to treat medical conditions such as glaucoma. However, this is a good example of more effective medicines already available. According to the Institute of Medicine, there are six classes of drugs and multiple surgical techniques that are available to treat glaucoma that effectively slow the progression of this disease by reducing high intraocular pressure.

• In other studies, smoked marijuana has been shown to cause a variety of health problems, including cancer, respiratory problems, loss of motor skills, and increased heart rate. Furthermore, marijuana can affect the immune system by impairing the ability of T-cells to fight off infections, demonstrating that marijuana can do more harm than good in people with already compromised immune systems.

• In addition, in a recent study by the Mayo Clinic, THC was shown to be less effective than standard treatments in helping cancer patients regain lost appetites.

• The American Medical Association recommends that marijuana remain a Schedule I controlled substance.

• The Drug Enforcement Administration (DEA) supports research into the safety and efficacy of THC (the major psychoactive component of marijuana), and such studies are ongoing, supported by grants from the National Institute on Drug Abuse.

• As a result of such research, a synthetic THC drug, Marinol, has been available to the public since 1985. The Food and Drug Administration has determined that Marinol is safe, effective, and has therapeutic benefits for use as a treatment for nausea and vomiting associated with cancer chemotherapy, and as a treatment of weight loss in patients with AIDS. However, it does not produce the harmful health effects associated with smoking marijuana.

• Furthermore, the DEA recently approved the University of California San Diego to undertake rigorous scientific studies to assess the safety and efficacy of cannabis compounds for treating certain debilitating medical conditions.

• It's also important to realize that the campaign to allow marijuana to be used as medicine is a tactical maneuver in an overall strategy to completely legalize all drugs. Pro-legalization groups have transformed the debate from decriminalizing drug use to one of compassion and care for people with serious diseases. The *New York Times* interviewed Ethan Nadelman, Director of the Lindesmith Center, in January 2000. Responding to criticism from former Drug Czar Barry McCaffrey that the medical marijuana issue is a stalking-horse for drug legalization, Mr. Nadelman did not contradict General McCaffrey. "Will it help lead toward marijuana legalization?" Mr. Nadelman said: "I hope so."

Additional dangers of marijuana

Does marijuana harm anyone besides the individual who smokes it?
• Consider the public safety of others when confronted with intoxicated drug users.

• Marijuana affects many skills required for safe driving: alertness, the ability to concentrate, coordination, and reaction time. These effects can last up to 24 hours after smoking marijuana. Marijuana use can make it difficult to judge distances and react to signals and signs on the road.

Users can become dependent on marijuana to the point they must seek treatment to stop abusing it.

• In a 1990 report, the National Transportation Safety Board studied 182 fatal truck accidents. It found that just as many of the accidents were caused by drivers using marijuana as were caused by alcohol—12.5 percent in each case.

• Consider also that drug use, including marijuana, contributes to crime. A large percentage of those arrested for crimes test positive for marijuana. Nationwide, 40 percent of adult males tested positive for marijuana at the time of their arrest.

Is marijuana a gateway drug?

• Yes. Among marijuana's most harmful consequences is its role in leading to the use of other illegal drugs like heroin and cocaine. Long-term studies of students who use drugs show that very few young people use other illegal drugs without first trying marijuana. While not all people who use marijuana go on to use other drugs, using marijuana sometimes lowers inhibitions about drug use and exposes users to a culture that encourages use of other drugs.

• The risk of using cocaine has been estimated to be more than 104 times greater for those who have tried marijuana than for those who have never tried it.

In summary:

• Marijuana is a dangerous, addictive drug that poses significant health threats to users.

• Marijuana has no medical value that can't be met more effectively by legal drugs.

• Marijuana users are far more likely to use other drugs like cocaine and heroin than non-marijuana users.

• Drug legalizers use "medical marijuana" as a red herring in an effort to advocate broader legalization of drug use.

2

Marijuana Is Relatively Harmless

Richard Lowry

Richard Lowry is editor of the National Review, *a conservative journal of opinion.*

Marijuana is a relatively innocuous drug, no more harmful than alcohol, tobacco, or caffeine. Most marijuana smokers are young adults who slow down or stop their drug use after the age of thirty-four, and the vast majority of these smokers do not go on to use other illicit drugs. Marijuana use can lead to mild psychological dependence, but the drug is not physically addictive. Long-term marijuana smokers may experience minor—but nonpermanent—cognitive impairments. The current illegal status of marijuana is rooted more in cultural prejudice than in truth: Alcohol and tobacco have been historically acceptable to Americans, while marijuana has been seen as an "alien" drug. Such prejudice does not justify prohibition.

Rarely do trial balloons burst so quickly. During the recent British campaign, Tory shadow home secretary Ann Widdecombe had no sooner proposed tougher penalties for marijuana possession than a third of her fellow Tory shadow-cabinet ministers admitted to past marijuana use. Widdecombe immediately had to back off. The controversy reflected a split in the party, with the confessors attempting to embarrass Widdecombe politically. But something deeper was at work as well: a nascent attempt to reckon honestly with a drug that has been widely used by baby boomers and their generational successors, a tentative step toward a squaring by the political class of its personal experience with the drastic government rhetoric and policies regarding marijuana.

The American debate hasn't yet reached such a juncture, even though the presidential campaign of 2000 featured one candidate who pointedly refused to answer questions about his past drug use and another who—according to Al Gore biographer Bill Turque—spent much of his young adulthood smoking dope and skipping through fields of clover (and still managed to become one of the most notoriously uptight and ambitious politicians in the country). In recent years, the debate over marijuana policy has centered on the question of whether the drug should be available for medicinal purposes. Drug warriors call medical marijuana the camel's nose under the tent for legalization, and so—for many of its advocates—it is. Both sides in the medical-marijuana controversy have ulterior motives, which suggests it may be time to stop debating the nose and move on to the full camel.

Already, there has been some action. About a dozen states have passed medical-marijuana laws in recent years, and California voters, in November 2000, approved Proposition 36, mandating treatment instead of criminal penalties for all first- and second-time nonviolent drug offenders. Proponents of the initiative plan to export it to Ohio, Michigan, and Florida in 2001. Most such liberalization measures fare well at the polls—California's passed with 61 percent of the vote—as long as they aren't perceived as going too far. Loosen, but don't legalize, seems to be the general public attitude, even as almost every politician still fears departing from former education secretary Bill Bennett orthodoxy on the issue. But listen carefully to the drug warriors, and you can hear some of them quietly reading marijuana out of the drug war. James Q. Wilson, for instance, perhaps the nation's most convincing advocate for drug prohibition, is careful to set marijuana aside from his arguments about the potentially ruinous effects of legalizing drugs.

There is good reason for this, since it makes little sense to send people to jail for using a drug that, in terms of its harmfulness, should be categorized somewhere between alcohol and tobacco on one hand and caffeine on the other. According to common estimates, alcohol and tobacco kill hundreds of thousands of people a year. In contrast, there is as a practical matter no such thing as a lethal overdose of marijuana. Yet federal law makes possessing a single joint punishable by up to a year in prison, and many states have similar penalties. There are about 700,000 marijuana arrests in the United States every year, roughly 80 percent for possession. Drug warriors have a strange relationship with these laws: They dispute the idea that anyone ever actually goes to prison for mere possession, but at the same time resist any suggestion that laws providing for exactly that should be struck from the books. So, in the end, one of the drug warriors' strongest arguments is that the laws they favor aren't enforced—we're all liberalizers now.

Marijuana use is nearly harmless

There has, of course, been a barrage of government-sponsored anti-marijuana propaganda over the last two decades, but the essential facts are clear: Marijuana is widely used, and for the vast majority of its users is nearly harmless and represents a temporary experiment or enthusiasm. A 1999 report by the Institute of Medicine—a highly credible outfit that is part of the National Academy of Sciences—found that "in 1996, 68.6 million people—32% of the U.S. population over 12 years old—had tried marijuana or hashish at least once in their lifetime, but only 5% were current users." The academic literature talks of "maturing out" of marijuana use the same way college kids grow out of backpacks and Friedrich Nietzsche. Most marijuana users are between the ages of 18 and 25, and use plummets after age 34, by which time children and mortgages have blunted the appeal of rolling paper and bongs. Authors Robert J. MacCoun and Peter Reuter—drug-war skeptics, but cautious ones—point out in their book *Drug War Heresies* that "among 26 to 34 year olds who had used the drug daily sometime in their life in 1994, only 22 percent reported that they had used it in the past year."

Marijuana prohibitionists have for a long time had trouble maintaining that marijuana itself is dangerous, so they instead have relied on a bank shot—marijuana's danger is that it leads to the use of drugs that are actually dangerous. This is a way to shovel all the effects of heroin and cocaine onto marijuana, a kind of drug-war McCarthyism. It is called the "gateway theory," and has been so thoroughly discredited that it is still dusted off only by the most tendentious of drug warriors. The theory's difficulty begins with a simple fact: Most people who use marijuana, even those who use it with moderate frequency, don't go on to use any other illegal drug. According to the Institute of Medicine report, "Of 34 to 35 year old men who had used marijuana 10–99 times by the age 24–25, 75% never used any other illicit drug." As Lynn Zimmer and John Morgan point out in their exhaustive book *Marijuana Myths/Marijuana Facts*, the rates of use of hard drugs have more to do with their fashionability than their connection to marijuana. In 1986, near the peak of the cocaine epidemic, 33 percent of high-school seniors who had used marijuana also had tried cocaine, but by 1994 only 14 percent of marijuana users had gone on to use cocaine.

Marijuana is widely used, and for the vast majority of its users is nearly harmless and represents a temporary experiment or enthusiasm.

Then, there is the basic faulty reasoning behind the gateway theory. Since marijuana is the most widely available and least dangerous illegal drug, it makes sense that people inclined to use other harder-to-find drugs will start with it first—but this tells us little or nothing about marijuana itself or about most of its users. It confuses temporality with causality. Because a cocaine addict used marijuana first doesn't mean he is on cocaine because he smoked marijuana (again, as a factual matter this hypothetical is extremely rare—about one in 100 marijuana users becomes a regular user of cocaine). Drug warriors recently have tried to argue that research showing that marijuana acts on the brain in a way vaguely similar to cocaine and heroin—plugging into the same receptors—proves that it somehow "primes" the brain for harder drugs. But alcohol has roughly the same action, and no one argues that Budweiser creates heroin addicts. "There is no evidence," says the Institute of Medicine study, "that marijuana serves as a stepping stone on the basis of its particular physiological effect."

The relationship between drugs and troubled teens appears to be the opposite of that posited by drug warriors—the trouble comes first, then the drugs (or, in other words, it's the kid, not the substance, who is the problem). The Institute of Medicine reports that "it is more likely that conduct disorders generally lead to substance abuse than the reverse." The British medical journal *The Lancet*—in a long, careful consideration of the marijuana literature—explains that heavy marijuana use is associated with leaving high school and having trouble getting a job, but that this association wanes "when statistical adjustments are made for the fact that, compared with their peers, heavy cannabis users have poor high-school performance before using cannabis." (And, remember, this is heavy use: "adolescents who casually experiment with cannabis," according to MacCoun and Reuter, "appear to function quite well with respect to schooling and mental health.") In the same way problem kids are attracted to illegal drugs, they are drawn to alcohol and tobacco. One study found that teenage boys who smoke cigarettes daily are about ten times likelier to be diagnosed with a psychiatric disorder than non-smoking teenage boys. By the drug warrior's logic, this means that tobacco causes mental illness.

Marijuana is not very addictive

Another arrow in the drug warriors' quiver is the number of people being treated for marijuana: If the drug is so innocuous, why do they seek, or need, treatment? Drug warriors cite figures that say that roughly 100,000 people enter drug-treatment programs every year primarily for marijuana use. But often, the punishment for getting busted for marijuana possession is treatment. According to one government study, in 1998 54 percent of people in state-run treatment programs for marijuana were sent there by the criminal-justice system. So, there is a circularity here: The drug war mandates marijuana treatment, then its advocates point to the fact of that treatment to justify the drug war. Also, people who test positive in employment urine tests often have to get treatment to keep their jobs, and panicked parents will often deliver their marijuana-smoking sons and daughters to treatment programs. This is not to deny that there is such a thing as marijuana dependence. According to *The Lancet*, "About one in ten of those who ever use cannabis become dependent on it at some time during their 4 or 5 years of heaviest use."

> *Most people who use marijuana, even those who use it with moderate frequency, don't go on to use any other illegal drug.*

But it is important to realize that dependence on marijuana—apparently a relatively mild psychological phenomenon—is entirely different from dependence on cocaine and heroin. Marijuana isn't particularly addictive. One key indicator of the addictiveness of other drugs is that lab rats will self-administer them. Rats simply won't self-administer THC, the active ingredient in marijuana. Two researchers in 1991 studied the addictiveness of caffeine, nicotine, alcohol, heroin, cocaine, and marijuana. Both ranked caffeine and marijuana as the least addictive. One gave the two drugs identical scores and another ranked marijuana as slightly less addicting than caffeine. A 1991 U.S. Department of Health and Human Services report to Congress states: "Given the large population of marijuana users and the infrequent reports of medical problems from stopping use, tolerance and dependence are not major issues at present." Indeed, no one is quite sure what marijuana treatment exactly is. As MacCoun and Reuter write, "Severity of addiction is modest enough that there is scarcely any research on treatment of marijuana dependence."

Dependence on marijuana—apparently a relatively mild psychological phenomenon—is entirely different from dependence on cocaine and heroin.

None of this is to say that marijuana is totally harmless. There is at least a little truth to the stereotype of the Cheech & Chong "stoner." Long-term heavy marijuana use doesn't, in the words of *The Lancet*, "produce the severe or grossly debilitating impairment of memory, attention, and cognitive function that is found with chronic heavy alcohol use," but it can impair cognitive functioning nonetheless: "These impairments are subtle, so it remains unclear how important they are for everyday functioning, and whether they are reversed after an extended period of abstinence." This, then, is the bottom-line harm of marijuana to its users: A small minority of people who smoke it may—by choice, as much as any addictive compulsion—eventually smoke enough of it for a long enough period of time to suffer impairments so subtle that they may not affect everyday functioning or be permanent. Arresting, let alone jailing, people for using such a drug seems outrageously disproportionate, which is why drug warriors are always so eager to deny that anyone ever goes to prison for it.

In this contention, the drug warriors are largely right. The fact is that the current regime is really only a half-step away from decriminalization. And despite all the heated rhetoric of the drug war, on marijuana there is a quasi-consensus: Legalizers think that marijuana laws shouldn't be on the books; prohibitionists think, in effect, that they shouldn't be enforced. A reasonable compromise would be a version of the Dutch model of decriminalization, removing criminal penalties for personal use of marijuana, but keeping the prohibition on street-trafficking and mass cultivation. Under such a scenario, laws for tobacco—an unhealthy drug that is quite addictive—and for marijuana would be heading toward a sort of middle ground, a regulatory regime that controls and discourages use but doesn't enlist law enforcement in that cause. MacCoun and Reuter have concluded from the experience of decriminalizing the possession of small amounts of marijuana in the Netherlands, twelve American states in the 1970s, and parts of Australia that "the available evidence suggests that simply removing the prohibition against possession does not increase cannabis use."

The cultural prejudice against marijuana

Drug warriors, of course, will have none of it. They support a drug-war Brezhnev doctrine under which no drug-war excess can ever be turned back—once a harsh law is on the books for marijuana possession, there it must remain lest the wrong "signal" be sent. "Drug use," as Bill Bennett has said, "is dangerous and immoral." But for the overwhelming majority of its users marijuana is not the least bit dangerous. (Marijuana's chief potential danger to others—its users driving while high—should, needless to say, continue to be treated as harshly as drunk driving.) As for the immorality of marijuana's use, it generally is immoral to break the law. But this is just another drug-war circularity: The marijuana laws create the occasion for this particular immorality. If it is on the basis of its effect—namely, intoxication—that Bennett considers marijuana immoral, then he has to explain why it's different from drunkenness, and why this particular sense of well-being should be banned in an America that is now the great mood-altering nation, with millions of people on Prozac and other drugs meant primarily to make them feel good.

In the end, marijuana prohibition basically relies on cultural prejudice. This is no small thing. Cultural prejudices are important. Alcohol and tobacco are woven into the very fabric of America. Marijuana doesn't have the equivalent of, say, the "brewer-patriot" Samuel Adams (its enthusiasts try to enlist George Washington, but he grew hemp instead of smoking it). Marijuana is an Eastern drug, and importantly for conservatives, many of its advocates over the years have looked and thought like [beatnik poet] Allen Ginsberg. But that isn't much of an argument for keeping it illegal, and if marijuana started out culturally alien, it certainly isn't anymore. No wonder drug warriors have to strain for medical and scientific reasons to justify its prohibition. But once all the misrepresentations and exaggerations are stripped away, the main pharmacological effect of marijuana is that it gets people high. Or as *The Lancet* puts it, "When used in a social setting, it may produce infectious laughter and talkativeness."

3

Long-Term Marijuana Use Is Not Harmful

I. Marwood

I. Marwood is a freelance writer.

Smoking marijuana is relaxing and pleasurably intoxicating. While it may make people act silly and spaced-out, marijuana does not cause aggression, oversentimentality, or hangovers as alcohol can. Many people from all walks of life smoke cannabis on a regular basis—with no serious adverse effects—and they are finding that today's marijuana is of higher quality than it was in the past. One rarely mentioned benefit of marijuana use is its effect on family life. Parents who smoke marijuana become less irritable and more childlike and therefore enjoy spending more time with their children.

I now divide my friends into two categories: those who smoke dope and those who don't get invited to my dinner parties. The last time I tried to mix the drinkers and the dopeheads, it was a huge flop. There came a point, at about midnight, when the drinkers got noisier and more argumentative, chain-smoked smelly cigarettes and wanted to crack open the whisky. The dope-smokers found this all a bit frightening. They just wanted to chill out, listen to the music, murmur about the meaning of life and then retire for an early night.

Me, I'm with the dope-smokers all the way. Though I like the odd drink, I'm invariably repelled by people who've had too much: their breath stinks, and their personalities change so that they become aggressive or maudlin. But that's one of the dangers of dope. The more you smoke, the less you want to drink, which can turn you into a bit of a prig.

Boozers often claim that dope-smoking makes you poor company. You sit around being vague and spaced-out, giggling inanely at non-existent jokes and spouting gibberish that is only comprehensible to people on the same weird planet as you. All I can say in our defence is that it doesn't seem that way to us at the time. As far as we're concerned, we're being as insightful and witty and clever as any mortal has ever been.

I. Marwood, "Absolutely Spliffing," *Spectator*, Vol. 283, August 21, 1999, p. 17. Copyright © 1999 by *Spectator*. Reproduced by permission.

It may well be that all those wondrous *aperçus*—'stoner insights'— turn out to be embarrassingly banal when recalled in the morning. But they're not nearly as embarrassing as the 'you're my besht friend' guff you come up with when you've had too many drinks. And dope doesn't give you a serious hangover, so you don't spend the morning-after racked with guilt and self-hatred.

Choosing marijuana

So if ever I had to choose between alcohol and marijuana—and Heaven forfend that I should—I'd plump for dope every time. Hence, no doubt, my dismay and astonishment when I chance upon statistics like the one cited in the *Daily Telegraph* in August 1999, that at least one in five Britons has at some time in their life dabbled with marijuana.

Good God, I thought. Who are these four in five people who have never tried a spliff? Are they madmen? Are they liars? Are they the product of some government propaganda department designed to persuade us that marijuana consumption remains the preserve of a few beatniks, hippies, crusties and other undesirables? Because, in my experience, it's the other way round. Roughly four in five of the people I know have smoked, and often continue to smoke, dope on a regular basis. It's those who don't that form the slightly eccentric minority.

[Dope-smokers just want] to chill out, listen to the music, murmur about the meaning of life and then retire for an early night.

The dope-smokers I know—many of them honest *Spectator*-reading folk—range in age from their teens to their sixties and include bankers, lawyers, policemen, doctors, entrepreneurs and blue-chip businessmen. But they're certainly not going to let on unless they can be sure that a) you won't disapprove or, preferably, b) you're going to whip out your secret stash of prize-winning Californian sinsemilla and bond with them over a celebratory reefer. That's the problem with being a 'head': you can only talk about your hobby with fellow heads.

Every time you pass a reefer to a friend, you are technically guilty of supply and liable to a caution, a fine or even a prison sentence. You can't smoke openly in bars, clubs, or indeed in any public place. And there are times—*pace* William Rees-Mogg's claim that in Somerset you can more easily buy dope than you can the *Spectator*—when it can be a devil of a job getting hold of your supplies, especially in the drought period before Christmas and the New Year.

Once you do get your hands on some, though, you will find that marijuana has rarely been better. Ten years ago, you usually had to make do with either feeble homegrown weed or dodgy imported hashish cut so heavily with unpleasant additives (sleeping tablets, melted down vinyl, etc.) that it either made you feel queasy or sent you to sleep. Now smokers' lives have been transformed by the wide availability of a new form of superweed, known as Skunk.

Skunk—once found only in Amsterdam, now grown in lofts all over Britain—is a hydroponically cultivated weed with big, pungent, compact floral heads and a smell exactly like that of a skunk. Many smokers, those who work for a living anyway, prefer to keep their stash of 'Make No Plans' Skunk for weekend-use only.

The first few puffs make you feel relaxed; the next few, lightheaded and pleasantly detached from reality; the next, garrulous, inspired and giggly. After that, the effects grow less predictable. As the Furry Freak Brothers say, 'Dope comes in two quantities: too much and not enough'. Personally, I tend to go through the horrors stage no more than two or three times a year: a small price to pay for the many, many other evenings where dope takes me to the sort of places alcohol can never reach.

Dope and family life

Another rarely cited virtue of dope is that it goes remarkably well with family life. I know many young mothers who would surely have strangled their bawling offspring by now had it not been for the numbing solace of a spliff. And though the same could be said of drink, dope doesn't impair your faculties to the same degree, so you can still function perfectly well as a nurturing parent.

Indeed, one remarkable side-effect I've noticed in dope is the way it makes children so much more interesting. Normally, I tend to find their conversation dull and irritating. But, after a few joints, one seems to have far more time and inclination to listen to their burblings; and perhaps even to go with them to marvel at the exciting wriggly worm or to join them for a session on their Sony Playstation. Perhaps it's because dope brings you down to their level and helps you rediscover your inner child. Or perhaps that's just the sort of hippie nonsense you'd expect an addled old head to come up with.

No, the only serious risk of dabbling with the wicked weed is that you're liable to become a bit of a drugs bore. There's nothing your average dope-smoker enjoys quite so much as discoursing on the respective merits of Durban Poison, Red-Bearded Skunk, pressed Moroccan pollen, charis, sinsemilla and Nepalese Temple Balls. I could go on, but better, surely, if you just go out and discover these pleasures for yourself. So skin up, turn on and chill out. You'll find yourself in excellent company.

4

Marijuana Is a Dangerous Drug for Teens

Joseph A. Califano Jr.

Joseph A. Califano Jr. is chair and president of the National Center on Addiction and Substance Abuse at Columbia University.

Marijuana is an especially harmful drug for children and adolescents. Marijuana can stunt a youth's intellectual, emotional, and psychological growth by impairing memory, learning abilities, and motor skills at crucial stages of human development. Furthermore, statistics have proven that marijuana is a gateway drug— people who smoke it are more likely than nonusers to try drugs such as cocaine, LSD, or heroin. While most youths who smoke marijuana may not move on to harder drugs, a significant percentage do—a fact that suggests that the best strategy in preventing drug abuse is to maintain strong social sanctions against marijuana. Efforts to decriminalize marijuana should therefore be opposed, and marijuana's potential for medical use should be clearly distinguished from the issue of legalizing the drug for the general population.

For certain individuals with AIDS and the 15 percent of chemotherapy patients whose nausea is not relieved by currently available medicines, marijuana may have some medicinal value. That is something to be determined by the research and clinical trials that the Institute of Medicine (IOM) recommended in its report, *Marijuana and Medicine: Assessing the Science Base*, issued in 1999. The risks and benefits of marijuana as medicine are matters for physicians, scientists, the National Institutes of Health, and the Food and Drug Administration. Because smoked marijuana is a carcinogen and adversely affects the immune system, the IOM stressed the importance of developing an alternative delivery system, such as an aerosol using synthetic cannabinoids rather than the whole plant, and disapproved any use of smoked marijuana except by the terminally ill and those in extremis with chronic diseases, and even then only under tightly controlled circumstances.

For America's children and teens, marijuana is a dangerous drug. The extent of the danger and the most effective way to keep our youngsters from using this drug are matters for teens, parents, schools, churches, communities and public policy makers.

For America's children and teens, marijuana is a dangerous drug.

Marijuana's potential as medicine, as the IOM report noted, has nothing to do with whether the drug should be made more widely available or its possession, cultivation and distribution should be legalized for the general population. That is the subject of this viewpoint, with special emphasis on the implications for children of legalization or decriminalization. Now that we know a child who gets through age 21 without smoking, using marijuana or any other illegal drug, or abusing alcohol is virtually certain never to do so, a key measure of any drug policy should be how well it helps achieve that objective.

Recent discussions of marijuana policy have failed to make this key distinction between marijuana as medicine and marijuana as recreation. President Lyndon Johnson used to say that the problem with the Democratic party was that the politicians want to be intellectuals and the intellectuals want to be politicians. Marijuana discussions suffer an analogous problem: too many politicians want to play scientist and too many scientists want to play politician. Marijuana legalization proponents like to play doctor and prescribe marijuana by political referendum. Many opponents of decriminalizing or legalizing marijuana also like to play physician, opposing scientific inquiry to determine whether the drug might have any medicinal value. Medical marijuana should not be the nose under the tent leading to the drug's general legalization (as some proponents hope) any more than the medical use of cocaine and opiates has been regarded as an opening move in the direction of general use. . . .

A dangerous drug for youth

The potential of marijuana as a dangerous drug for our children, as a gateway to other drug use, and as a signal of trouble is a matter of the most serious concern for American parents. And there's plenty to justify such parental concern:

• *Smoking marijuana, in and of itself, is especially dangerous for teens.* The drug can impair short term memory, ability to concentrate and motor skills at a time when these are particularly important to children developing and learning in school. Marijuana can stunt the intellectual, emotional and psychological development of adolescents. In some ways, marijuana combines the adverse health effects of both our currently legal drugs: the intoxication of alcohol with the lung damage of tobacco. Nine percent of those who ever use marijuana become dependent on it. In 1996 (the latest year for which numbers are available), more than 195,000 individuals entered treatment for marijuana; 62 percent (more than 120,000) of whom are under age 25, 45 percent (nearly 88,000) are teens or younger. There are more teens and children in treatment for marijuana than for any other substance including alcohol.

    • *Statistically speaking, marijuana stands convicted as a gateway drug.* Twelve- to 17-year-olds who smoke marijuana are 85 times more likely to use cocaine than those who do not. Among teens who report no other problem behaviors, those who used cigarettes, alcohol and marijuana at least once in the past month are almost 17 times likelier to use another drug like cocaine, heroin or LSD. To appreciate the power of these statistical relationships, remember that the 1964 Surgeon General's report on Smoking and Health found a nine to ten times greater risk of lung cancer among smokers; the early results of the Framingham heart study found individuals with high cholesterol two to four times likelier to get heart disease; and the Selikoff study found that workers exposed to asbestos were five times likelier to get lung cancer.

There are more teens and children in treatment for marijuana than for any other substance including alcohol.

    Biomedical and scientific studies are beginning to unearth the reason for this tight statistical relationship between use of marijuana and other drugs. Recent studies at universities in California, Italy and Spain reveal that marijuana affects levels of dopamine (the substance that gives pleasure) in the brain in a manner similar to heroin and cocaine (as well as nicotine and alcohol). While scientists have not yet uncovered the smoking gun, they have certainly found the trigger finger. Proponents of decriminalization and legalization argue that so long as there is not conclusive proof of the gateway relationship, we should not worry about it. But parents who mistake the absence of proof for the proof of absence are playing Russian Roulette with their children's lives. Although most kids who use marijuana will not move on to heroin and cocaine, teens who use marijuana are far more likely to get into harder drugs than teens who don't. Remember, most cigarette smokers will not get lung cancer; less than 20 percent will.

Decriminalization would increase use by teens

    • *Decriminalization for all ages of possession of small amounts of marijuana (e.g., an ounce, enough for 40 to 50 joints) or legalization of use, cultivation and distribution of the drug will increase use by adolescents.*

    We've been there, done that.

    In the early 1960s a few hundred thousand individuals had smoked marijuana. Decriminalization, more lenient laws, and lax enforcement of existing state and federal laws opened the way for an enormous surge in use that peaked in 1979 when 30 million Americans smoked marijuana.

    • *Decriminalization or legalization of marijuana only for adults will increase use by minors.*

    We've been there, done that, too.

    The sale of two legal recreational drugs, alcohol and tobacco, is prohibited for those under 18 (for tobacco) and under 21 (for alcohol). Use of these drugs by adolescents far exceeds their use of marijuana which is illegal for all regardless of age. Of high school tenth graders (usually 15 to 16 years old), nearly 28 percent have smoked cigarettes and 39 percent have used alcohol in the past month—in contrast, 19 percent have smoked marijuana. Among younger students, use of alcohol and nicotine is also substantially higher than marijuana use. Of eighth graders, 23 percent drank and 19 percent smoked during the past month—in contrast, 10 percent have smoked marijuana.

Smoking marijuana is not a rite of passage, but a very decidedly dangerous game of Russian Roulette.

The Center on Addiction and Substance Abuse (CASA) White Paper, *Non-Medical Marijuana: Rite of Passage or Russian Roulette?*, makes clear that decriminalization or legalization of the drug would certainly increase use among the nation's teens and children. In a society that looks to government to protect it from unsafe cars and toys—and that recognizes that the availability of guns increases likelihood of their use—it is hard to understand why anyone would take actions likely to make this drug more readily available to our children.

Sending a clear message

Clearly, there ought to be a law. For teens, laws prohibiting the possession, distribution and cultivation of marijuana send a clear signal that smoking pot is dangerous and a conduct that society strongly disapproves.

This is not to say that all drug policies and laws on the books make sense. Laws that prescribe mandatory sentences for possession of small amounts of marijuana are overkill. In general, mandatory sentences, especially those requiring drug and alcohol abusers and addicts to serve their entire sentence, are counterproductive. We need all the carrots and sticks we can muster to help these individuals shake their habit. Mandatory sentences take away any potential that an early release might hold as an incentive for such an inmate to enter treatment. Such sentences also remove the leverage that parole officers need to get recently released inmates to continue treatment and aftercare or face a return to prison.

Mandatory sentences are particularly insidious where teens convicted of possession of marijuana are concerned. In such cases, prosecutors and judges should be given wide discretion in order to encourage the teen to stop using the drug. The best chance of achieving that objective is to permit prosecutors and judges to set a punishment proportionate to the offense, for they are positioned to know what sanctions and opportunities are most likely to get the youngster back on track. The early results from the drug courts attest to the value of giving judges and prosecutors wide discretion in dealing with defendants.

At bottom, we must all recognize that the most important influences on children and teens are parents, relatives, friends, teachers, coaches, clergy and community. It is across the kitchen table, in the school yard, church pew and neighborhood that the problem of teen drug use will be resolved. Those who most influence teens—parents, friends, teachers, coaches, clergy—are helped by the clear signal that laws prohibiting possession, distribution and cultivation of marijuana send. Such laws provide support outside the home for the guidance that teens receive from their parents inside the home. As the IOM report on medical marijuana and a host of work sponsored by the National Institute on Drug Abuse of the National Institutes of Health indicate, smoking marijuana is a decidedly dangerous pastime for anyone, just on the basis of its adverse health implications.

Teen experimentation with marijuana should not be considered a casual rite of passage. Teens who smoke marijuana are playing a dangerous game of Russian Roulette. Most kids who smoke pot will not move on to cocaine, heroin and acid, but those who do smoke it greatly hike the odds that they will use harder drugs. Not all kids who smoke pot will become dependent on the drug, but nine percent will. Not all kids who smoke pot will go into drug treatment to try and shake the habit, but nearly 88,000 of the 195,000 individuals undergoing such treatment are teens and children and more teens and children are in treatment for marijuana than for any other drug, including alcohol. Not all kids who experiment will become regular users or pot heads but the only sure way to avoid that is not to smoke marijuana. Not all kids who smoke marijuana will so severely impair their short term memory and ability to concentrate that they will fail in school, drop out or seriously arrest their intellectual development, but many will. Not all teens who get high on marijuana will be involved in a crippling or killing auto accident, but getting high greatly increases the dangers of driving and getting high is the reason teens (and adults) smoke pot. Society, through its laws and customs, has an obligation to do all it can to support parents and others who understand that smoking marijuana is not a rite of passage, but a very decidedly dangerous game of Russian Roulette.

There is more than enough evidence that decriminalization or legalization of marijuana would greatly increase the danger that our children would use this drug. That is reason enough to reject any such course of action. The one thing our teens—and our society—do not need is a third legal drug.

5

Marijuana Is Not an Exceptionally Dangerous Drug for Teens

Marsha Rosenbaum

Marsha Rosenbaum is a medical sociologist who has written numerous books, scholarly articles, and editorials about drug use, drug treatment, and drug policy. This viewpoint is exerpted from her booklet Safety First: A Reality-Based Approach to Teens, Drugs, and Drug Education.

Many teenagers experiment with marijuana in high school, and the vast majority of them suffer no ill effects. Young people today are bombarded with messages that encourage the use of numerous symptom-reducing or mind-altering substances, including over-the-counter and prescription drugs, so teen experimentation with illegal drugs should not be seen as deviant. While parents and teachers should work to prevent serious drug abuse among teens, they should avoid educational programs that rely on scare tactics and misinformation about the effects of marijuana. Because teenagers know from their own experience that marijuana is relatively harmless, exaggerating the harms of marijuana makes it more likely that they will ignore messages about the dangers of harder drugs.

L ike many parents, when my children entered adolescence, I wished "the drug thing" would magically disappear and my children would simply abstain. But as a drug abuse expert whose research was funded by the National Institute on Drug Abuse, and as a parent in the 90s, I knew this wish to be a fantasy. Despite expected federal expenditures of more than $2.2 billion on drug use prevention in 2002 and five to seven times that at the state and local levels, government surveys indicate that most teenagers experiment with drugs before they graduate from high school. In the words of L.D. Johnston et al., "According to the most recent *Monitoring the Future* survey, 53.9% of high school seniors experimented with illegal drugs at some point in their lifetime; 41.4% used a drug during the past year [2001]; and 25.7% used drugs in the past month."

Marsha Rosenbaum, *Safety First: A Reality-Based Approach to Teens, Drugs, and Drug Education*, San Francisco, CA: Drug Policy Alliance, 2002. Copyright © 2002 by Drug Policy Alliance. Reproduced by permission.

Most youthful drug use is experimental, and fortunately, the vast majority of young people get through adolescence unscathed. Still, I worry about those whose experimentation gets out of hand, who fall into abusive patterns with drugs and put themselves and others in harm's way.

Today's adolescents have been exposed, since elementary school, to the most intensive and expensive anti-drug campaign in history. Haven't they been told, again and again, to "just say no" by school-based programs such as Drug Abuse Resistance Education (DARE)? Why aren't they listening? What, if anything, can we do about it? How might we, as parents and teachers, be educating our teenagers more effectively? Is there anything we can do to better ensure their safety?

Most youthful drug use is experimental, and fortunately, the vast majority of young people get through adolescence unscathed.

As a parent, I urgently wanted to know the answers to these questions, so I consulted with experts—including teachers, parents and young people, themselves. I also looked at drug education, its history, curricula and existing evaluations. The result was the 1999 edition of *Safety First: A Reality-Based Approach to Teens, Drugs, and Drug Education*.

I did not set out to criticize particular programs. On the contrary, I wanted to understand what might be missing from their content, and how we might accomplish the prevention of drug problems more productively. I hoped to help other parents, as well as teachers and school administrators.

Since releasing the first edition in 1999, more than 30,000 copies have been distributed to individuals and educational, health and governmental institutions in all 50 states, Puerto Rico, the District of Columbia and around the world. In addition, I have made dozens of presentations and spoken with hundreds of parents, teachers and students. The feedback received over the past several years shaped the 2002 edition of *Safety First*.

Drug education strategies

Education to prevent drug use has existed in America for over a century. A variety of methods—from scare tactics to resistance techniques—have been used with the intention of encouraging young people to refrain from drug use altogether. Despite the expansion of these abstinence-only programs, it is difficult to know which, if any, are actually successful.

More than half of all high school students in America experiment with illegal drugs, and even more use alcohol. They see for themselves that America is hardly "drug-free." They know there are differences between experimentation, abuse and addiction; and that the use of one drug does not inevitably lead to the use of others. Adolescence is also a time for trying new things and taking risks.

Yet, conventional drug education programs focus predominantly on abstinence-only messages and are shaped by problematic myths:

- *Myth #1:* Experimentation with drugs is not a common part of teen-age culture;
- *Myth #2:* Drug use is the same as drug abuse;
- *Myth #3:* Marijuana is the gateway to drugs such as heroin and co-caine; and
- *Myth #4:* Exaggerating risks will deter young people from experi-mentation.

Teenagers make their own choices about drugs and alcohol, just as we did. Like us, they sometimes make foolish mistakes. However, since we can-not be there to protect them 100 percent of the time, we have to find ways to trust them when they are not under our watch. It is our responsibility as parents and teachers to engage young people in dialogue, listen to them, and provide a sounding board and resources when they need our help.

Abstinence may be what we'd all prefer for our youth, but this sim-plistic goal may not be attainable. Our current efforts lack harm reduction education for those students who won't "just say no." In order to prevent drug abuse and drug problems among teenagers who do experiment, we need a fallback strategy that puts safety first.

Educational efforts should acknowledge teens' ability to sort through complex issues and make decisions that will ensure their own safety. The programs should offer credible information, differentiate between use and abuse, and stress the importance of moderation and context. Curric-ula should be age-specific, stress student participation and provide objec-tive, science-based materials. . . .

Teenage experimentation with legal and illegal mind-altering substances is not deviant.

Existing programs seem to send mixed messages; blur the lines be-tween use and abuse; use scare tactics; promote misinformation; and un-dermine the credibility of parents and teachers who provide this false in-formation. Too often, abstinence-only programs ignore young people's exposure to drug use and fail to engage them in a meaningful way.

Mixed messages

Despite proclamations about the value of being "drug-free," the American people and their children are perpetually bombarded with messages that encourage them to imbibe and medicate with a variety of substances such as alcohol, tobacco, caffeine and over-the-counter and prescription drugs.

The *Journal of the American Medical Association* recently reported that 8 out of 10 adults in the U.S. used at least one medication every week, and half took a prescription drug. Nearly one in two American adults use al-cohol regularly; and more than one-third have tried marijuana at some time in their lives—a fact not lost on their children.

Today's teenagers have also witnessed the increasing "Ritalinization" of their fellow difficult-to-manage students. And as they watch prime-time commercials for drugs to manage "Generalized Anxiety Disorder," they see more of their parents turning to anti-depressants to cope.

Teenage drug use seems to mirror modern American drug-taking tendencies. Therefore, some psychologists argue, given the nature of our culture, teenage experimentation with legal and illegal mind-altering substances is not deviant.

Use and abuse

Adults routinely make distinctions between use and abuse. While growing up, young people rapidly learn the difference, too. Most observe their parents and other adults using alcohol (itself a drug) without abusing it. Many also know that their parents, at some point in their lives, used an illegal drug (usually marijuana) without becoming abusers.

Teenagers know from their own experience and observation that marijuana use does not inevitably, or even usually, lead to the use of harder drugs.

In an effort to prevent teenage experimentation, too often programs pretend there is no difference between use and abuse. Some use the terms interchangeably; others emphasize an exaggerated definition of use that categorizes any use of illegal drugs or anything other than one-time experimentation as abuse.

Programs that blur the distinctions undermine educational efforts because students' own experiences tell them the information presented is not believable. As one 17-year-old girl, an 11th-grader in Fort Worth, Texas, put it, *"They told my little sister that you'd get addicted to marijuana the first time, and it's not like that. You hear that, and then you do it, and you say, 'Ah, they lied to me.'"*

Although there is nothing more frightening than a teenager whose use of alcohol and/or other drugs gets out of hand and becomes a problem, virtually all studies have found that the vast majority of students who try drugs do not become abusers. As parents, we can be more effective in dealing with problem use if we are clear and fair about the distinctions.

Scare tactics and misinformation

A common belief among many educators, policy makers and parents is that if teenagers simply believe that drug experimentation is dangerous, they will abstain. As a result, many prevention programs include exaggerated risk and danger messages. Although the old *Reefer Madness*–style messages have been replaced by assertions that we now have scientific evidence of the dangers of drugs, the evidence, particularly about marijuana, just isn't there. When these studies are critically evaluated, few of the most common assertions hold up.

I first realized the dangers of using scare tactics 25 years ago, while working on my doctoral dissertation about heroin addiction. One of my first interviews was with a "nice Jewish girl," like myself; from an affluent suburb in a large metropolitan area. Genuinely intrigued by the different turns our lives had taken, I asked how she had ended up addicted to heroin and in jail. I will never forget what she told me:

> *"When I was in high school they had these so-called drug educa-tion classes. They told us if we used marijuana we would be come addicted. They told us if we used heroin we would become ad-dicted. Well, we all tried marijuana and found we did not become addicted. We figured the entire message must be B.S. So I tried heroin, used it again and again, got strung out and here I am."*

Marijuana, the most popular illegal drug among teens, is routinely demonized in abstinence-only messages. Many Web sites, including those managed by the federal government, include misinformation about mar-ijuana's potency, its relationship to cancer, memory, the immune system, personality alteration, addiction and sexual dysfunction.

In *Marijuana Myths, Marijuana Facts: A Review of the Scientific Evidence,* Professor Lynn Zimmer and Dr. John P. Morgan carefully examined the scientific evidence relevant to each of these alleged dangers. They found, in essentially every case, that the claims of marijuana's dangerousness did not hold up. Their findings are not uncommon. Over the years, the same conclusions have been reached by numerous official commissions, in-cluding the La Guardia Commission in 1944, the National Commission on Marijuana and Drug Abuse in 1972, the National Academy of Sciences in 1982, and, in 1999, the Institute of Medicine.

A frightening ramification of imparting misinformation is that like the heroin addict I interviewed 25 years ago, teenagers will ignore our warnings completely and put themselves in real danger. The increased purity and availability of "hard" drugs and teenagers' refusal to heed warnings they don't trust, have resulted in increased risk of fatal over-dose, such as those we've witnessed among the children of celebrities and in affluent communities.

Another case in point is Ecstasy. Despite a $5 million media cam-paign to alert young people to its dangers, year after year, government surveys indicate a rise in its use. When I ask teenage users why they have not heeded government warnings, they express deep cynicism. Said one 18-year-old regarding problematic brain changes attributed to Ecstasy, *"Oh yes, they told us about that with marijuana, too. But none of us believes we have holes in our brains, so we just laugh at those messages."*

The gateway theory

The gateway theory, a mainstay of drug education, suggests that mari-juana use leads to the use of harder drugs such as cocaine and heroin. There is no credible research evidence demonstrating that using one drug causes the use of another.

For example, a large survey conducted by the federal government shows that the vast majority of marijuana users do not progress to the use of more dangerous drugs. Based on the National Institute on Drug Abuse *Household Survey,* Zimmer and Morgan calculated that for every 100 people who have tried marijuana, only one is a current user of cocaine. A recent analysis based on the same survey and published in the prestigious *American Journal of Public Health* and a report issued by the Institute of

Medicine, also refuted the gateway theory.

Teenagers know from their own experience and observation that marijuana use does not inevitably, or even usually, lead to the use of harder drugs. In fact, the majority of teens who try marijuana do not even use marijuana itself on a regular basis. Therefore, when such information is presented, students discount both the message and the messenger.

The consistent mischaracterization of marijuana may be the Achilles heel of current approaches to prevention, because such misinformation is inconsistent with students' own observations and experience. As a result, teenagers lose confidence in what we, as parents and teachers, tell them. In turn, they are less likely to consider us credible sources of information.

6

Marijuana Has Medical Value

Lester Grinspoon

Lester Grinspoon is Associate Professor Emeritus of psychiatry at Harvard Medical School.

Cannabis has long been recognized as an effective medicinal. In the nineteenth century, solutions containing cannabis were used to relieve pain and induce sleep. Early in the twentieth century, the medical attractiveness of marijuana waned as a disinformation campaign against its recreational use spread. After the 1970s, the medical uses of cannabis were rediscovered when patients undergoing chemotherapy found that smoking marijuana relieved the nausea and vomiting that are common side effects of the treatment. Currently, marijuana has been found useful in treating glaucoma, AIDS wasting syndrome, osteoarthritis, convulsive disorders, and other chronic ailments. The government and the mainstream medical community, however, overestimate the dangers of marijuana smoke and are reluctant to make it available as a prescribed medicine. Although cannabis derivatives are legally obtainable in pill form, many patients find smokable marijuana more effective—and less expensive. The American public will eventually learn that the dangers of marijuana have been overstated and will demand changes in its legal status.

Cannabis—also known as *Cannabis sativa,* hemp, and marijuana—first became a part of Western pharmacopoeias 150 years ago. In 1839, W.B. O'Shaughnessy of the Medical College of Calcutta observed its use in traditional Indian treatment of various disorders and found that tincture of hemp was effective as an analgesic, an anticonvulsant, and a muscle relaxant. In the next several decades, many papers on cannabis appeared in Western medical journals. And it was in widespread medical use in the West, especially as an analgesic and a hypnotic (sleep inducer), until the early 1900s. Symptoms and conditions for which cannabis was found helpful included asthma, convulsions, dysmenorrhea, labor pain, neuralgia, rheumatism, and tetanus. In the heyday of Western medical use of

Lester Grinspoon, "Reefer Sanity," *Priorities for Health*, Vol. 13, 2001, pp. 33–39. Copyright © 2001 by The American Council on Science and Health. Reproduced by permission.

cannabis, physicians in the West generally administered it as a tincture (alcoholic solution), which was typically referred to as "tincture of hemp," "tincture of cannabis," or "Cannabis indica" (the species name "indica" means "of or relating to India"). Physicians did not know that smoking cannabis would have brought relief sooner than did ingesting its tincture. Moreover, the variance of tincture of hemp, in terms of potency and bioavailability, was considerable, and no reliable bioassay techniques existed. Nevertheless, physicians prescribed it without much concern about overdosing or side effects. On the other hand, they with good reason considered cannabis less reliable as an analgesic than opium or its derivatives. And unlike such drugs, the bioactive principles of cannabis are insoluble in water and are thus totally unsuitable for administration by injection.

At the turn of the 19th century, both aspirin (the first manmade analgesic) and the first barbiturate became available. These drugs attracted physicians immediately, because their potencies were fixed and their administration was simple. From the 1920s, as the medical attractiveness of cannabis continued to fall, interest in it as an aid to recreation—and a disinformation campaign against such use—grew. In 1937 came the first draconian federal enactment against marijuana use: the Marijuana Tax Act, which made prescribing marijuana so cumbersome that most physicians abandoned its medical use. And with an editorial published in *The Journal of the American Medical Association* in 1945 began the medical establishment's becoming one of the most effective agents of cannabis prohibition.

The re-medicalizing of marijuana

The revival of cannabis as a medicinal began in the early 1970s, when several young subjects of new modes of cancer chemotherapy found that smoking marijuana was much more effective than were conventional treatments in relieving nausea and vomiting. These are side effects of some anticancer drugs and as such can be intense and lasting. Word of these patients' experience with marijuana spread quickly over the cancer-treatment grapevine. By the middle of the decade the capacity of marijuana to lower pressure inside the eyeball was observed, and patients with glaucoma (which is characterized by abnormally high intraocular pressure) began to try it as a treatment for this disorder. And as the AIDS epidemic snowballed, many patients wasting because of HIV infection found that smoking marijuana was both more effective in preventing weight loss and less troubling in terms of side effects than were conventional treatments for this life-threatening symptom.

Cannabis has currently been found useful against some 30 symptoms and syndromes.

These uses of cannabis have led to wider health-related folk uses of the plant, and its utility in the symptomatic treatment of convulsive disorders, migraine, insomnia, and dysmenorrhea has been rediscovered. Indeed, cannabis has currently been found useful against some 30 symptoms and syndromes. And many patients regard smoking marijuana as more effective, and as having a smaller downside, than conventional treatments for those of their health problems against which they are using the drug. Osteoarthritis is a case in point. In the 19th century tincture of cannabis was often used to treat the pain of osteoarthritis. Shortly after its introduction, aspirin—one of the early non-steroidal anti-inflammatory drugs, or NSAIDs—displaced cannabis as the treatment of choice for osteoarthritic and many other types of non-intense pain. But NSAIDs are responsible for the loss of about 10,000 American lives annually, while cannabis has never been demonstrably responsible for the death of anyone using it—irrespective of one's reason for using it. Moreover, the pain relief that smoking cannabis brings can be better than that of NSAIDs, and unlike NSAIDs, cannabis can improve the mood of those who use it. Thus, it should surprise no one that many patients with osteoarthritis treat its pain with cannabis.

"Pot-pourri"

Apparently, the number of Americans who understand the medical utility of cannabis has increased in the last few years. This positive interest has been marked politically by the passage in nine states of initiatives or legislation to permit limited use of cannabis as a medicine. The enactment of such legislation has led to a clash with federal authorities who recently were blasting the medical usage of marijuana as a hoax. Under public pressure to acknowledge the medical potential of marijuana, Barry McCaffrey—the director of the Office of National Drug Policy—authorized a review by the Institute of Medicine (IOM) of the National Academy of Sciences. In its report of this review, published in March 1999, the IOM admitted, restrainedly, that cannabis had medical value.

But the IOM stated that smoking is too dangerous a mode of drug delivery for cannabis—a conclusion based on an overestimate of the toxicity of marijuana smoke. Among its major recommendations was that patients with "debilitating symptoms (such as intractable pain or vomiting)" be permitted to smoke marijuana only after all conventional treatment options have failed—and then, only for six months and under "an oversight strategy comparable to an institutional review board process." Following this recommendation would make the legal use of cannabis unworkable in most clinical settings. It seems that the IOM would have patients who find cannabis healthful when they smoke it await, for years, introduction of a mode of drug delivery for cannabis that does not involve smoking the drug. Devices are in development that take advantage of the fact that cannabinoids vaporize at temperatures below the ignition point of marijuana.

The IOM report treats marijuana—a versatile drug with a long history and low toxicity—as if it were comparable to thalidomide, a drug whose possible side effects include phocomelia (a severe birth defect) and whose medical utility is limited to Hansen's disease (leprosy) and multiple myeloma (a type of bone cancer). But at least the report confirms that even U.S. government officials recognize the medical utility of cannabis. The development of cannabinoids into lawful treatment options for various symptoms and conditions appears inevitable. Chiefly in question is how cannabinoids will be administered.

Schedules and agendas

It was in the early 1970s that I first considered the issue of legalizing the use of marijuana in medical practice. Then, I assumed that the cannabis used medically would be the same as that used recreationally, which typically consisted of the dried flowering tops of female *Cannabis indica* plants. I assumed so partly because such material had minimal toxicity and would have been inexpensive if it weren't prohibited. I thought the main obstacle to medical use of marijuana was its classification in Schedule I of the Comprehensive Drug Abuse and Control Act of 1970, which describes it as (*a*) having a high potential for being abused, (*b*) having no accepted medical use, and (*c*) lacking safety for administration even under medical supervision. American physicians could not (and cannot) legally prescribe Schedule I drugs, which include heroin and LSD. In those days, I believed that making marijuana a Schedule II drug would greatly facilitate the legal availability of marijuana as a medicine. I had come to believe that prohibition of marijuana, not the drug itself, was responsible for the greatest harm in using marijuana recreationally. But I saw the prohibition of recreational use of marijuana as an issue independent from that of its medical use. The use of opiates and cocaine as restricted medicines was lawful, while all other uses were unlawful. I reasoned that the cannabis situation should be no different. I thought that categorizing marijuana as a Schedule II drug would fast result in the eager pursuit of clinical research on it in the U.S. More than 25 years later I came to doubt this eventuality.

On the whole, patients evidently find smoking marijuana more effective than taking manmade THC.

The Drug Enforcement Administration (DEA) treats Schedule II drugs, which include cocaine and morphine, as having some medical utility but also a high potential for being abused. Thus, making marijuana a Schedule II drug would not be an adequate measure for making it available as a prescription medication. Among the prerequisites for FDA approval of any drug as a prescription product is rigorous, expensive, time-consuming testing of the drug.

The FDA's approval process was designed to regulate the commercial distribution of pharmaceutical-company products and to defend the public against false or misleading claims about pharmaceutical-product safety and efficacy. In general, the product subjected to this process is a single manmade chemical that a pharmaceutical company has developed and patented. According to this process, the pharmaceutical company submits an application to the FDA; tests its product for safety in laboratory animals and then for safety and efficacy in humans; and presents evidence from double-blind controlled studies that the product is significantly more effective than a placebo—and at least as effective as drugs legally on the market in the U.S.—against the ailment or symptom for which the product was developed. Case studies, the opinions of experts, and clinical experience are unimportant in this process. The cost to pharmaceutical companies for putting a product completely through it exceeds $200 million per drug. It is unlikely that any marijuana product designed to be smoked will ever become an officially recognized medicine by this means.

The extensive government-supported campaign of the last three decades to generate and publicize evidence that cannabis is toxic enough to call for its drastic prohibition has furnished a record of safety for the drug that is more encouraging than the safety record of most FDA-approved medicines. To require that subjecting smokable cannabis to the process described above precede its legal medical use is like requiring the same for aspirin—which was in widely accepted medical use in Europe and the U.S. more than 60 years before the advent of the double-blind controlled study. That aspirin is versatile and of low toxicity has been known clinically for many years. But marshaling aspirin through the FDA's drug-approval process would be improbable—only because its patent has expired. Cannabis, too, is unpatentable, and, under the current protocol, there is little or no incentive to invest in seeking FDA approval of anything unpatentable. So the only potential funder for subjecting cannabis to the FDA's approval process is the federal government of the United States, which—in light of America's anti-smoking climate and the prevalence in the U.S. of nonmedical uses of cannabis that the government condemns—is extremely unlikely to fund such studies.

Stumbling blocks

Permitting particular medical uses of marijuana while trying to prevent any other use would be difficult. Then there is the question of how cannabis would be provided. Under a program in phaseout, the federal government supplies marijuana grown on its farm in Mississippi to eight patients. But the federal government has never been in the business of producing any prescription drug for thousands of patients and is very unlikely to do so, especially if the drug is marijuana. If the government contracted with nongovernmental farmers to produce marijuana, security might be costly. Other important questions include those stated below.

- If pharmacies filled cannabis prescriptions, protecting the drug in terms of freshness and thievery would become an extra burden for them.
- The federal government might delimit prices for pharmaceutical marijuana. If the prices to patients are too high, they might provoke patients' buying cannabis from pushers or growing it on their own. If they're too low, they might prompt consumers' besieging physicians for cannabis prescriptions on the purported basis of dubious or trifling health problems.
- Testing an individual's urine for controlled substances or illicit drugs yields no information on whether the individual used the chemical legally.

In the current sociopolitical climate, to legitimize cannabis as a prescription medicine in the U.S. would prerequire exploring each of the matters stated above, and others. And any system of cannabis legitimization that might emerge from such an exploration would be cumbersome, inefficient, and top-heavy. Governmental bodies and medical licensing boards would demand tight restrictions on the prescribing of cannabis, challenging any physician who does so whenever a patient first receives a prescription for it or receives the prescription on a diagnostic basis new to him. Consequently, many patients likely to benefit from the medical use of marijuana would settle for their benefiting suboptimally from its medical availability, whereas many other patients of this kind would obtain the drug from the black market or from their own gardens.

Cannabinoids

According to one of the major current proposals that bear on making the dichotomization of cannabis use effective, lawful cannabis prescriptions would be restricted to isolated natural cannabinoids (THC and other derivatives of *Cannabis sativa*), manmade cannabinoids, and analogs (close structural relatives) of cannabinoids. The IOM report states that "if there is any future for marijuana as a medicine," it lies in cannibinoids and analogs of such. It further states: "Therefore, the purpose of clinical trials of smoked marijuana would not be to develop marijuana as a licensed drug, but such trials could be a first step towards the development of rapid-onset, non-smoked cannabinoid delivery systems."

Ultimately, whether any cannabis-related medicinal becomes a commercial success will depend on the degree to which authorities try to enforce the ban on traditional marijuana.

In certain circumstances, taking isolated cannabinoids and/or analogs of them may be more advantageous than smoking or ingesting marijuana. For example, ingesting cannabidiol without other constituents of marijuana may be more effective in reducing anxiety than is ingesting it with THC—a cannabinoid that sometimes causes anxiety. Analogs of cannabinoids may prove more medically useful than smoked marijuana at least partly because they can be safely administered into veins. An example is dexanabinol (HU-211). In 15–20 percent of cases of thrombotic or embolic stroke, loss of consciousness ensues. Such also ensues in some persons who sustain a severe blow to the head resulting in a brain syndrome. In both of these situations, dexanabinol has proved protective of brain cells—and that it can be safely introduced into veins is a big plus. It is presumable that other cannabinoid analogs have advantages over the dried leaves and/or dried flowers of *Cannabis sativa*. And any cannabinoid or analog thereof that has none of the effects that make marijuana desirable as an aid to recreation would not fall under the constraints of the Comprehensive Drug Abuse and Control Act. Further, cannabinoids and their analogs could be administered in a way that does not entail smoking anything (e.g., as an aerosol or by suppository or transdermal patch). Inhalation is a very effective means of administering cannabinoids, and except for injection there are no means of getting cannabinoid analogs to function sooner. Vaporization devices can separate cannabinoids in marijuana from burnt marijuana, and mass production would make such devices inexpensive. It is dubitable, however, whether the availability of nonsmokable cannabis-related medicinals would render pot smoking unfit or superfluous as a medical treatment.

The American public would eventually learn that the harmfulness of marijuana was greatly exaggerated and its utility underestimated.

Moreover, although doubtless there could be many such medicinals useful enough and safe enough for commercial development, it is not certain that pharmaceutical companies would consider most of them worthy of the costs of seeking FDA approval. It might be lucrative to subject to this approval process, say, a cannabinoid that could reduce the desire to eat. But against any definite symptom, using cannabinoid analogs—singly or in combination—is unlikely to be more effective than smoking cannabis. For example, on the whole, patients evidently find smoking marijuana more effective than taking manmade THC (known as Marinol or Dronabinol), which has been available for years.

Under the current system, any analog without a therapeutic ratio (a safety rating) acceptable to the FDA would not become legally available outside medical research. Because evidently no one has ever died directly because of ingesting or smoking marijuana, its therapeutic ratio is unknown, but from animal-experiment data it has been extrapolated at 20,000 to 40,000. It is unlikely that any new cannabinoid analog would rate higher. Indeed, such an analog might be less safe than smoked marijuana—simply because one can take cannabis-related chemicals more efficiently by swallowing pills than by smoking marijuana.

Psychoactive cannabinoid analogs would fall under the constraints of the Comprehensive Drug Abuse and Control Act. The more restrictive the law is concerning a specific type of drug, the less likely a pharmaceutical company will develop—and the less likely a physician will prescribe—any drug of that type. Unimed attained FDA approval of the exorbitantly expensive drug Marinol relatively inexpensively only because Marinol was identical to the marijuana constituent THC and the U.S. government had underwritten much of the cost. And although Marinol has been recategorized from Schedule II to Schedule III, it is almost certain that, for fear of the DEA, physicians will continue refusing to prescribe it.

Ultimately, whether any cannabis-related medicinal becomes a commercial success will depend on the degree to which authorities try to enforce the ban on traditional marijuana. Almost certainly, such medicinals will cost much more than does traditional marijuana, even with its prohibition-inflated prices. I doubt that any pharmaceutical company would be inclined to develop cannabic products if it had to compete on a level playing field with street vendors of marijuana. The general illegality of marijuana in the U.S. is the commonest reason for taking Marinol. Many patients smoke street marijuana instead of taking Marinol because they find smoked marijuana more effective and because marijuana is less expensive than Marinol.

There is little doubt that pharmaceutical companies will develop useful cannabis-related products, some of which may not fall under the constraints of the Comprehensive Drug Abuse and Control Act. But, in my opinion, it is unlikely that such products will replace traditional marijuana as a medicine. Many Americans use it as such despite that arrests on marijuana-related charges in the U.S. have steadily increased to 700,000 annually.

The bottom line

Two major forces are in opposition: the growing acceptance of cannabis as a remedy worthy of mainstream medical approval, and the blanket proscription of marijuana. Two very different distribution pathways for cannabis-related products may emerge from this conflict: one conventional, with pharmacies filling prescriptions for FDA-approved cannabis-related products; the other similar to that of ethnic medicinals and herbal and other dietary supplements, except that marijuana would continue to be prohibited. The coexistence of these pathways would result in an increase both in the medical use of cannabis and in the number of persons who are familiar with cannabis and its derivatives. In my opinion, the American public would eventually learn that the harmfulness of marijuana was greatly exaggerated and its utility underestimated—and would therefore demand drastic change in how institutions and regulatory agencies deal with its use.

7

The Medical Value of Marijuana Has Been Overstated

Robert L. Maginnis

Robert L. Maginnis is the vice president for national security and foreign affairs at the Family Research Council, a conservative educational and lobbying organization. In 1999 he was appointed by Republican Senator Trent Lott to serve on the national Parents Advisory Council on Drug Abuse.

THC, the active ingredient in marijuana, has been found to have some medicinal properties. However, recent scientific studies reveal that marijuana's dangers greatly outweigh its benefits. Smokable marijuana is a harmful, unpredictable, and addictive substance that can cause or contribute to mental health problems, cardiovascular disease, cancer, and immune system disorders. For this reason, most scientific and medical authorities caution against the use of marijuana as medicine. Allowing marijuana to be used medicinally would also increase drug abuse—especially among teenagers—and create more social and law enforcement problems. The real agenda of most medical marijuana advocates, moreover, is legalization of the drug for the general population—not just for the sick.

The debate over the "medical" usefulness of marijuana should have been settled with the 1999 publication of a study by the Institute of Medicine (IOM). The findings from that government-sponsored study are outlined in the *Insight* paper, "Bad Medicine and Drug Legalization: A 2000 Update." One of the most damaging conclusions was that "marijuana's future as a medicine does not require smoking." Unfortunately, marijuana advocates have dismissed that report and the volumes of respected scientific studies that prove marijuana's dangers.

In spite of anecdotally based "medical" marijuana advocacy, the science against marijuana as "medicine" or as a recreational drug continues

Robert L. Maginnis, "Marijuana Is Bad Medicine: 2001 Update," www.frc.org, 2001. Copyright © 2001 by Family Research Council. Reproduced by permission.

to mount. The following summarizes what the scientific community has published about marijuana since early 2000.

Marijuana's addictive properties

• *Marijuana withdrawal symptoms identified.* The November 2000 issue of *Experimental and Clinical Psychopharmacology* reports that researchers have identified marijuana withdrawal symptoms as significant in 60 percent of study participants. "Most people think marijuana is a benign drug, and there is disagreement in the scientific community about whether withdrawal causes significant symptoms," said Dr. Elena M. Kouri, the study's author and associate director of the McLean Behavioral Psychopharmacology Research Laboratory in Virginia. Kouri continued, "This study shows that marijuana [use] for a long time has consequences." The study reports that marijuana withdrawal includes increases in irritability, anxiety and physical tension, as well as decreases in appetite and mood.

• *Marijuana acts like other addictive drugs in animal trials.* Scientists at the National Institute on Drug Abuse (NIDA) have demonstrated that laboratory animals will self-administer marijuana's psychoactive component, THC (delta-9-tetrahydrocannabinol), in doses equivalent to those used by humans who smoke the drug. Self-administration of drugs by animals, long considered a model of human drug-seeking behavior, is characteristic of virtually all addictive and abused drugs. Dr. Steven Goldberg, an NIDA researcher who was published in the journal *Nature Neuroscience*, said that "squirrel monkeys will self-administer intravenous injections of THC." Goldberg continued, "This finding suggests that marijuana has as much potential for abuse as other drugs of abuse, such as cocaine and heroin."

• *Most marijuana addicts need extensive help recovering.* A year 2000 study by Australia's National Drug and Alcohol Research Center (NDARC) found that only 10 percent of cannabis (marijuana) addicts were able to stop using the drug after a series of counseling sessions. Dr. Wendy Swift, one of the study's researchers, said that "many clients expressed depression, they also attributed problems with concentration and memory, isolating themselves from others, and lack of motivation to their cannabis use." The study's dependent cannabis users spent an average of 27 percent of their income on the drug. They began smoking cannabis at the age of fifteen and on average had used the drug for fourteen years.

A 1999 NDARC report found that 31.7 percent of cannabis users were dependent. The most commonly reported dependence symptoms were a persistent desire for cannabis, unsuccessful efforts to moderate use (36.6 percent) and withdrawal symptoms (29.7 percent).

Marijuana's dangerous health effects

• *Marijuana is a dangerous substance.* A February 2001 article in *The British Journal of Psychiatry* states that cannabis (marijuana) use can "cause dose-related impairments of psychomotor performance with implications for car and train driving, aeroplane piloting and academic performance." Marijuana cigarettes can be as addictive as nicotine, and the tars from marijuana contain higher levels of some cancer-causing chemicals than tobacco. Additionally, smoking three or four marijuana joints a day can

produce the same risk of bronchitis or emphysema as twenty or more tobacco cigarettes.

• *Marijuana-related emergency room visits rising.* A 1999 Drug Abuse
Warning Network report found that visits to the hospital emergency de-
partments because of marijuana use have risen steadily during the 1990s
from an estimated 15,706 visits in 1990 to 87,150 in 1999—a 455 percent
increase. Patients thirty-five years old or older experienced the largest increase in marijuana mentions (1,078 percent, from 2,160 to 25,453) from
1990 to 1999. Among children between the ages of twelve and seventeen,
marijuana mentions increased 489 percent (from 2,170 to 12,784) over
the same period.

• *Marijuana is linked to mental health problems.* A February 2001 article
in *The British Journal of Psychiatry* states that regular use of marijuana may
make things worse for people who have mental health problems. Andrew
Johns of the Institute of Psychiatry in London found that 15 percent of
marijuana users exhibited psychotic symptoms or irrational feelings of
persecution. Johns found that "an appreciable proportion of cannabis
users report short-lived adverse effects, including psychotic states following heavy consumption, and regular users are at risk of dependence.
People with major mental illnesses such as schizophrenia are especially
vulnerable in that cannabis generally provokes relapse and aggravates existing symptoms."

> *In spite of anecdotally based "medical" marijuana
> advocacy, the science against marijuana as
> "medicine" or as a recreational drug continues to
> mount.*

• *Pregnant marijuana users risk having children more prone to misbehav-
ior.* A May–June 2000 study in *Neurotoxicology and Teratology* found that
prenatal marijuana exposure has an effect on child behavior problems at
age ten. The behavior problems include increased hyperactivity, impul-
sivity, inattentiveness, increased delinquency, and externalization of
problems.

• *Marijuana use elevates risk of heart attack.* Smoking marijuana significantly elevates the risk of a heart attack. On March 6, 2000, Dr. Murray
Mittleman of the Harvard School of Public Health told an American Heart
Association conference that marijuana-smoking baby boomers are at increased risk of coronary artery disease. Mittleman's study found that the
risk of a heart attack is five times higher than usual in the hour following
the smoking of a joint. The researcher said that for someone in good
shape, marijuana is about twice as risky as exercising or having sex.

• *Marijuana use linked to cancers of the head and neck.* A December 1999
article in *Cancer Epidemiology Biomarkers & Prevention* found a link between marijuana use and cancerous tumors of the head and neck. The authors state, "this is the first epidemiological report that marijuana smoking is associated with a dose-dependent increased risk of head and neck
cancer. This association is supported by a series of case reports and by experimental studies that provide a biologically plausible basis for the hy-

pothesis that marijuana is a risk factor for head and neck cancer."

• *Some smokers are at higher risk of colorectal cancer.* The December 2000 issue of *Molecular Genetics and Metabolism* included a study that found that smokers with a pre-existing genetic mutation in the gene for alpha-1 anti-trypsin, which is linked to emphysema, could be twenty times more likely to develop colorectal cancer than those without the mutation. Dr. Ping Yang, a clinical epidemiologist at the Mayo Clinic in Rochester, Minnesota, warned that "smokers should be aware that their risk of lung cancer and heart disease is elevated, and so is their risk of colorectal cancer."

Sociology of marijuana use

• *Study develops taxonomy of marijuana users.* A May 2000 study in the *Journal of Studies on Alcohol* set out to develop a taxonomy of marijuana users. Four marijuana use clusters were identified: early onset–heavy use, early onset–light use, mid onset–heavy use and late onset–light use. The researchers found that, early onset into marijuana use does not necessarily lead to problematic use or rapid progression into the use of other drugs. They conclude, "motivation underlying use and dysfunctional behaviors are associated with the development of problematic drug use and dependence." Four risk factors have been found to be salient in the development of adolescent substance abuse: (1) poor parenting, particularly lack of monitoring and low closeness; (2) parental drug use; (3) association with a drug-using peer group; and (4) the child's prior behavioral difficulties and delinquency.

Regular use of marijuana may make things worse for people who have mental health problems.

• *Study asserts that marijuana is not necessarily a "gateway" drug.* A February 2001 study in the *American Journal of Public Health* examined the probabilities of progression that youthful substance use typically follows, use of alcohol or tobacco, and potentially proceeding to marijuana and then hard drugs. The study used data from the National Household Survey on Drug Abuse (1979 to 1997) and concluded that the "dire predictions of future hard drug abuse by youths who came of age in the 1990s may be greatly over-stated." The authors admit that the preponderance of studies replicating the gateway theory "might be a reliable foundation for guiding prevention policy and practice." However, the study says the gateway theory appears to reflect "norms prevailing among youths at a specific place and time and that the linkages between stages are far from causal."

Marijuana as "medicine"

It has been demonstrated that THC has medicinal value for some disease symptoms. Although the Food and Drug Administration has approved a synthetic THC tablet called Marinol® to provide relief for symptoms of certain ailments, there are questions about its utility. Some patients with

AIDS wasting and nausea associated with chemotherapy treatment have difficulty digesting the THC tablet. To help alleviate this problem, efforts are underway to provide improved means for delivering THC and to search for alternative drugs to THC.

• *FDA approves development of THC applications.* On May 11, 2000, the FDA approved clinical trials for CT-3, a synthetic derivative of THC. Atlantic Technology Ventures, Inc., has been approved to conduct clinical trials for CT-3, an analgesic and anti-inflammatory drug. Atlantic plans to develop oral and injectable versions of the compound for pain and inflammation associated with a variety of disease states. Additionally, on January 10, 2000, the *Associated Press* reported that the American Cancer Society has given a $361,000 grant to fund research into a THC patch.

• *Study finds "anti-vomiting" receptor for cancer treatments.* A 2000 article in *Neuropsychopharmacology* reports that an "anti-vomiting" receptor has been found that may offer a better understanding of marijuana's potential medicinal benefit. Nissar Darmani, with the Kirksville College of Osteopathic Medicine in Missouri, contends that he has located a receptor for marijuana. This may help scientists to develop cannabinoid drugs that can reduce the nausea and vomiting caused by radiation and chemotherapy while avoiding the "high" associated with marijuana.

Marijuana-smoking baby boomers are at increased risk of coronary artery disease.

The scientific community has identified a number of additional cautions about the use of marijuana as "medicine."

• *THC can promote tumor growth.* The July 2000 issue of *The Journal of Immunology* found that THC could promote tumor growth by impairing the body's anti-tumor immunity system. The study's authors suggest that smoking marijuana may be more of a cancer risk than smoking tobacco. The tar portion of marijuana smoke, compared to that of tobacco, contains higher concentrations of carcinogenic hydrocarbons, including benzopyrene, a key factor in promoting human lung cancer. Marijuana smoke deposits four times as much tar in the respiratory tract as does a comparable amount of tobacco, thus increasing exposure to carcinogens.

• *THC suppresses the immune system.* A 2000 study in *The Journal of Immunology* found that marijuana's THC suppresses immunity against legionella pneumophila (bacteria that causes legionnaire's disease).

• *Australian organization raises key concerns about marijuana as "medicine."* An Australian organization called the "Working Party on the Use of Cannabis for Medical Purposes" responded to an August 2000 study entitled "Use of Cannabis for Medical Purposes." The Working Party's response included an observation about the variability of THC in cannabis, and it also included the following expert statements:

• *Cannabis is a very unpredictable "medicine."* John Malouf, a spokesman for Australian Pharmacists Against Drug Abuse, stated, "Cannabis sativa must be one of the most controversial drugs of all time. Botanically it is a very unstable species with over a hundred plant varieties of differing strengths. . . . This basic botanical fact has been ignored by many who discuss the drug as if it were a single substance with mild intoxicant properties. Its unpredictable nature varies immensely from individual to individual and according to the strength of the product used."

- *Cannabis can be dangerous for depressed patients.* Dr. Garry Pearce, with the New South Wales (Australia) Multiple Sclerosis (MS) Society, said:

    The effect of cannabis on MS from psychological and emotional aspects are not known and one suspects that as there is something like a seven times higher suicide rate in MS compared to the general population due to depression and as it is known that cannabis can exacerbate depression in susceptible people that this is another area that is likely to be exacerbated if cannabis was freely available on prescription for conditions such as MS.

- *Cannabis use associated with psychotic illness.* Ivan B. Lang, a colonel with the Salvation Army Australia Eastern Territory, stated:

    Between 1993 and 1997 there had been an almost 10 percent increase in the number of cannabis-dependent patients suffering from a drug-induced psychotic illness. A patient suffering from psychosis loses contact with reality, hears voices or sees things that are not there; his thoughts are confused. The available evidence tends to explode the myth that cannabis is a harmless drug.

Marijuana remains popular among vulnerable children

A key concern among drug use preventionists has been the link between pro-drug media messages and adolescent use. A recent study confirms that effective anti-drug messages do influence adolescents. Conversely, it is just as likely that drug use increases as media outlets glamorize drugs.

A February 2001 study in the *American Journal of Public Health* evaluated the effectiveness of targeted televised public service announcement campaigns in reducing marijuana use among sensation-seeking adolescents. The study found that PSAs could significantly reduce substance use in this high-risk population. Researchers report that campaigns with an anti-marijuana use message resulted in at least a 26.7 percent drop in the use of that drug among the targeted teen population. The targeted teens were defined as sensation seeking, "a personality trait associated with the need for novel, emotionally intense stimuli and the willingness to take risks to obtain such stimulation."

The growing attention given to marijuana in the media and especially in states that have hosted "medical" marijuana referenda perhaps explains increased drug use and decreased perception of risk among vulnerable adolescents. These trends have been especially pronounced over the past decade, the period of the upsurge in "medical" marijuana initiatives.

The year 2000 federal government–funded Monitoring the Future annual adolescent drug-use survey found the following increases in lifetime (once or twice) prevalence use of marijuana between 1991 and 2000:

- Eighth-graders from 10.2 percent in 1991 to 20.3 percent in 2000,
- Tenth-graders from 23.4 percent in 1991 to 40.3 percent in 2000, and
- Twelfth-graders from 36.7 percent in 1991 to 48.8 percent in 2000. Annual use is somewhat lower by grade: 16 percent of eighth-graders, 32 percent of tenth-graders, and 37 percent of twelfth-graders.

Not surprisingly, this survey found that the perception of risk from marijuana continues its downward trend. Among those who have tried marijuana once or twice, the perception of harmfulness has declined:

- Among eighth-graders from 40.4 percent in 1991 to 29 percent in 2000,
- Among tenth-graders from 30 percent in 1991 to 18.5 percent in 2000, and
- Among twelfth-graders from 27.1 percent in 1991 to 13.7 percent in 2000.

Government studies confirm that when the perception of risk goes down, use goes up.

In 1999, the percentages of adolescent (ages twelve to seventeen) and young adult (ages eighteen to twenty-five) state residents reporting use of marijuana within the preceding month tended to be highest in those states that have passed "medical" marijuana laws. The national average was 7.9 percent for adolescents and 14.7 percent for young adults.

The increase in "medical" marijuana initiatives has accompanied a similar increase in the first-time use of marijuana by adolescents (ages twelve to seventeen). Specifically, according to the 1999 National Household Survey, the rates of marijuana initiation for youth during 1995 through 1998 (the period of most "medical" marijuana referenda) are at their highest levels since the peak levels in the late 1970s.

The rise in first-time marijuana use and the declining perception of risk associated with marijuana should disturb parents and lawmakers. Lawmakers can propose some remedies but parents are the first line of defense against drug abuse. Two recent studies point to good parenting as the best antidote to drug use.

"The available evidence tends to explode the myth that cannabis is a harmless drug."

A March 2000 study in the *American Journal of Public Health* examined the dynamic patterns and predictors of marijuana use onset. The authors conclude that (1) the risk of initiation spans the entire course of adolescent development; (2) young people exposed to others who use substances are at higher risk for early initiation; (3) proactive parents can help delay initiation; and (4) clear family standards and proactive family management are important in delaying marijuana use.

A February 2001 study by the Center on Addiction and Substance Abuse at Columbia University found that adolescents with "hands-on" parents have a substantially lower risk of drug use than the average teen. The study found only one in four teens (27 percent) lives with "hands-on" parents, however. "Hands-on" parenting means a parent monitors his teen's television and Internet viewing, restricts the CDs the teen purchases, knows where his teen is after school and on weekends, imposes a curfew, has dinner with his teen six or seven times a week, closely monitors his teen's academic performance, and gives his teen a clear message about marijuana use.

The increase in "medical" marijuana initiatives has accompanied a similar increase in the first-time use of marijuana by adolescents.

The survey noted that religious activity "is a significant factor in that teen's risk" of substance abuse. Those teens in the survey who never attend religious services had above-average risk of drug use, according to the survey, while the teens who attended services weekly (or more often) had a substantially lower risk of drug use. . . .

The latest twists on "medical" marijuana enforcement

Law enforcement in states with "medical" marijuana laws faces very unique challenges.

Medical marijuana supporters in California mount recall campaigns of prosecutors who target marijuana users. Paula Kamena, a first-term district attorney in Marin County, said, "If you possess an amount consistent with personal use, we don't prosecute. If you are a woman with breast cancer or an AIDS patient, we don't prosecute." In spite of this lenient attitude, Kamena is accused of harassing medical marijuana users. She faces a voter recall. Five medical marijuana-related recall campaigns are expected this year [2001] in California.

Local jurisdictions have created special legal "carve outs," which compromise law enforcement. Santa Cruz, California approved an ordinance sanctioning medicinal marijuana collectives that provide free pot to members whose illnesses could be aided by the illicit drug. The law sanctions the Wo/Men's Alliance for Medical Marijuana, a collective based in the Santa Cruz Mountains whose two-hundred members suffer from cancer, AIDS, epilepsy and other ailments.

Efforts to protect "medical" marijuana doctors from law enforcement: In March 2000, the Santa Cruz city council unanimously approved an ordinance allowing medical marijuana to be grown and used without a prescription. This protects doctors from federal prosecution who might recommend marijuana as medicine.

On July 17, 2000, a San Francisco federal judge barred federal officials from interfering with California doctors' and patients' ability to discuss the medical benefits of marijuana. This decision came in a class action lawsuit filed against the federal government, seeking to block it from prosecuting or removing the prescription licenses of any doctor who endorsed marijuana for medicine.

Some medical doctors flagrantly abuse the "medical" marijuana loophole. A December 22, 2000, paid advertisement in the *Oakland Tribune* read: "Medical Marijuana Physician Evaluations." The advertisement promised physician evaluations for "any other condition for which marijuana provides relief" such as "menstrual/bowel/muscle cramps, insomnia, hepatitis C/HIV discomforts, neuropathy, fibromyalgia, TMJ, asthma, constipation, nausea etc."

Law enforcement must read the fine print. In 1999, Maine voters approved a straightforward "medical" marijuana law. In December 2000, police were called to the home of Charles Wynott because of an argument. Incident to that call, police found Wynott in possession of a baggie of marijuana. He protested that it was used as medicine for AIDS. He presented a letter from his physician, but his physician is in Florida and now Wynott lives in Maine. Maine's "medical" marijuana law requires a letter from a doctor licensed in Maine.

How much marijuana is enough? Vancouver, Washington paramedics responded to a 911 call to the home of Steven Pogue, an AIDS patient who also suffers from dementia. Incident to the visit, police found marijuana plants growing in the bathroom. Pogue has a doctor's recommendation to smoke marijuana to ease his pain and restore his appetite. Not knowing whether the plants violated a "legal" sixty-day supply for medicinal purposes, the police confiscated the plants and the growing equipment. Pogue filed a claim against the city. Vancouver officials agreed to pay Pogue $5,000 to settle the case.

Diverting "medical" marijuana. Peter Baez, who founded Santa Clara County California's first medical marijuana center, plea-bargained seven felony drug counts. He was charged with illegally selling marijuana outside the center. He pled no contest to selling marijuana but received no jail time.

Diversion of "medical" marijuana is a serious problem. The Berkeley California Community Health Commission is trying to decide how much pot is enough. The commission has proposed allowing one hundred forty-four plants for a patient who grows them indoors and sixty plants for one who grows them outdoors. Police department representative Lieutenant Russell Lopes wants the number reduced. He worries that cultivating large numbers of plants by personal growers would encourage home robberies. "There were six home-invasion robberies last year directly related to residents who had large amounts of marijuana in the house," Lopes said. "While we support a medical marijuana ordinance, we see an inherent risk in allowing large amounts to be grown in the home."

Free-flowing marijuana, whether for "medical" purposes or recreational purposes, will add to the drug's growing contribution to traffic accidents.

Marijuana frequently implicated in auto accidents. Free-flowing marijuana, whether for "medical" purposes or recreational purposes, will add to the drug's growing contribution to traffic accidents. An April 2000 review of two National Highway Traffic Safety Administration studies found that alcohol remains the predominant drug in fatal crashes, but marijuana is the drug next most frequently found in drivers involved in crashes. Both alcohol and marijuana are often found together in drivers involved in motor vehicle crashes. A 1996 National Household Survey of Drug Abuse found that more than one fourth of the 166 million drivers age sixteen and older occasionally drive under the influence of alcohol, marijuana, or both. Marijuana, even in low to moderate doses, negatively affects driving performance in real traffic situations. Under marijuana's influence, drivers have reduced capacity to avoid collisions if confronted with the sudden need for evasive action.

Those pushing marijuana as "medicine" continue to expose their real objective: outright drug legalization.

Marijuana use is often associated with sexual assault victims. A May 2000 study published in the *Journal of Reproductive Medicine* found a strong relationship between substance abuse and sexual assault. Urine samples taken from victims of sexual assault found alcohol in 63 percent of the samples and marijuana in 30 percent.

The "red herring" of drug policy

Those pushing marijuana as "medicine" continue to expose their real objective: outright drug legalization. Decades ago, Keith Stroup, the executive director for the National Organization for Reform of Marijuana Laws (NORML) labeled "medical" marijuana the "red herring" for outright drug legalization.

Not surprisingly, a number of radical drug policy referenda have followed close on the heels of successful "medical" marijuana initiatives. Predictably, the same people who financed the recent "medical" marijuana referenda have funded these initiatives.

Wealthy entrepreneurs with pro-drug views have bankrolled most of these initiatives. Three gentlemen in particular have consistently financed these initiatives: George Soros, a New York investor and philanthropist, Peter B. Lewis, the CEO of the Progressive Corporation (an Ohio insurance company), and John Sperling of Arizona, founder of the University of Phoenix. These men have provided the vast majority of the financing for these initiatives either directly or through Americans for Medical Rights, a front organization pushing for looser drug laws. There is evidence that at least one of these men may have a personal interest in changing the drug laws. On January 10, 2000, *The Washington Times* reported that Peter Lewis was arrested in New Zealand. He admitted to three charges of importing drugs after customs officers found two ounces of hashish and 1.7 ounces of cannabis in his luggage.

In the year 2000, there were examples of the new trend in drug laws.

Attempt in Alaska to legalize pot use failed. In November 2000, the people of Alaska soundly defeated (60.7 percent against) Ballot Measure 5, which would have fully legalized marijuana. This initiative came only two years after passage of that state's successful "medical" marijuana initiative. The proposed initiative would have eliminated penalties for possession, use, cultivation and sale of marijuana.

California passed a radical drug law. Perhaps the most controversial drug initiative was California's Proposition 36, known as the "Substance Abuse and Crime Prevention Act." It passed (60.8 percent in favor). The initiative, which takes effect in the summer of 2001, mandates that drug offenders receive treatment, not prison time, for the first and second non-violent drug offenses. Unfortunately, Prop-36 may undermine the effectiveness of the successful drug court system. These courts maintain judicial control over non-violent offenders who volunteer to participate in treatment, submit to frequent drug tests and satisfy other behavior and work requirements in lieu of incarceration. The threat of jail gives the judge the needed power to keep many of his charges in the program. Prop-36 removes the threat of jail for first and second time offenders.

Massachusetts's voters narrowly defeated an initiative similar to Prop-36. On November 7, 2000, Massachusetts voters narrowly defeated (53 percent v. 47 percent) The Fair Treatment Initiative, which would have substituted treatment for incarceration for first and second time drug offenders. The pro-drug trio of Soros, Lewis and Sperling created the state organization called Coalition for Fair Treatment to run the unsuccessful campaign.

America is at a crossroads. If the "medical" marijuana laws aren't struck down by the Supreme Court in 2001, expect efforts to further radicalize drug laws. [In May 2001 the Supreme Court barred a medical-necessity exemption to the federal law criminalizing marijuana. This still leaves open the possibility that Congress could revise the federal law.] Such changes would ignore the science that proves the dangers of marijuana, no doubt fuel more use by children, frustrate law enforcement, and accelerate the social costs associated with drug abuse.

8

Marijuana Use Should Be Decriminalized

R. Keith Stroup

R. Keith Stroup is founder and executive director of the National Organization for the Reform of Marijuana Laws (NORML), an organization that advocates the legalization of marijuana.

Marijuana prohibition began in the 1930s, after its recreational use had become associated with minority immigrants and musicians. The U. S government launched a misinformation campaign against the drug, spreading exaggerations and lies about its effects, and passed a law that criminalized marijuana use. The continued prohibition of the drug by the government today is a destructive policy that wastes law enforcement resources and results in the needless arrests of thousands of productive and otherwise law-abiding citizens. When used responsibly by adults, marijuana is as safe and enjoyable as alcohol. Congress should decriminalize marijuana (that is, remove all penalties for its responsible use by adults) and allow individuals the freedom to choose how they would like to relax.

The National Organization for the Reform of Marijuana Laws (NORML) has been a voice for nearly 30 years for Americans who oppose marijuana prohibition. A nonprofit, public-interest lobby, NORML represents the interests of the millions of otherwise law-abiding citizens who smoke marijuana responsibly.

The official NORML position

(a) Complete decriminalization. NORML supports the removal of all penalties for the private possession and responsible use of marijuana by adults, cultivation for personal use, and the casual nonprofit transfers of small amounts. This model, generally called "decriminalization," greatly reduces the harm caused by marijuana prohibition by protecting millions of consumers from the threat of criminal arrest and jail. It represents a

R. Keith Stroup, testimony before the Subcommittee on Criminal Justice, Drug Policy and Human Resources, Committee on Government Reform, House of Representatives, July 13, 1999.

cease fire in the war against marijuana smokers; smokers would no longer be arrested, although commercial sellers would be.

(b) Regulation and legalization. NORML also supports the development of a legally controlled market for marijuana, where consumers could buy marijuana for personal use from a safe, legal source. This model is generally called "legalization." The black market in marijuana, and the attendant problems of crime and violence associated with an uncontrolled and unregulated black market, could be eliminated, as was the case when alcohol prohibition was ended in 1933, by providing consumers with an alternative legal market.

(c) Responsible use. Most importantly, marijuana smoking is not for kids and must be used responsibly by adults. As with alcohol consumption, it can never be an excuse for misconduct or other bad behavior. Driving or operating heavy equipment while impaired from marijuana should be prohibited. In addition, we recommend that responsible smokers adhere to emerging tobacco smoking protocols in public and private settings. The NORML Board of Directors has adopted the "Principles of Responsible Cannabis Use", available on our web site (www.norml.org), discussing acceptable conduct.

A brief history of marijuana prohibition

Marijuana cultivation in the United States can trace its lineage some 400 years. For most of our nation's history, farmers grew marijuana—then known exclusively as hemp—for its fiber content. Colonialists planted the first American hemp crop in 1611 near Jamestown, Virginia. Soon after, King James I of Britain ordered settlers to engage in wide scale farming of the plant. Most of the sails and ropes on colonial ships were made from hemp as were many of the colonists' bibles, clothing, and maps.

According to some historians, George Washington and Thomas Jefferson cultivated marijuana and advocated a hemp-based economy. Some colonies even made hemp cultivation compulsory, calling its production necessary for the "wealth and protection of the country." Marijuana cultivation continued as an agricultural staple in America through the turn of the 20th century.

> *Congress needs to move beyond the "reefer madness" phase of our marijuana policy.*

Marijuana first earned recognition as an intoxicant in the 1920s and 1930s. Recreational use of the drug became associated primarily with Mexican-American immigrant workers and the African-American jazz musician community. During this time, hemp was renamed "marihuana" and the plant's longstanding history as a cash crop was replaced with a new image: "The Devil's Weed."

In 1930, the federal government founded the Federal Bureau of Narcotics (FBN), headed by Commissioner Harry Anslinger. The group launched a misinformation campaign against the drug and enrolled the services of Hollywood and several tabloid newspapers. Headlines across the nation began publicizing alleged reports of marijuana-induced insanity and violence. Exaggerated accounts of violent crimes committed by immigrants reportedly intoxicated by marijuana became popularized. Once under the influence of the drug, criminals purportedly knew no fear and lost all inhibitions. For example, a news bulletin issued by the FBN in the mid-1930s purported that a user of marijuana "becomes a fiend with savage or 'cave man' tendencies. His sex desires are aroused and some of the most horrible crimes result. He hears light and sees sound. To get away from it, he suddenly becomes violent and may kill."

We certainly know marijuana is relatively safe when used responsibly by adults.

Similar reports swept the country. A widely publicized issue of the *Journal of Criminal Law and Criminology* asserted that marijuana users are capable of "great feats of strength and endurance, during which no fatigue is felt. . . . Sexual desires are stimulated and may lead to unnatural acts, such as indecent exposure and rape. . . . [Use of marijuana] ends in the destruction of brain tissues and nerve centers, and does irreparable damage. If continued, the inevitable result is insanity, which those familiar with it describe as absolutely incurable, and, without exception ending in death." A *Washington Times* editorial published shortly before Congress held its first hearing on the issue argued: "The fatal marihuana cigarette must be recognized as a deadly drug and American children must be protected against it." This steady stream of propaganda influenced 27 states to pass laws against marijuana in the years leading up to federal prohibition and set the stage both culturally and politically for the passage of the "Marihuana Tax Act in 1937."

Rep. Robert L. Doughton of North Carolina introduced the Act in Congress on April 14, 1937 to criminalize the recreational use of marijuana through prohibitive taxation. The bill was the brainchild of Commissioner Anslinger who later testified before Congress in support of the bill.

Congress held only two hearings, totaling one hour of testimony, to debate the merits of marijuana prohibition. Federal witness Harry Anslinger testified before the House Ways and Means Committee that "this drug is entirely the monster-Hyde, the harmful effect of which cannot be measured." He was joined by Assistant General Counsel for the Department of the Treasury, Clinton Hester, who affirmed that the drug's eventual effect on the user "is deadly." These statements summarized the federal government's official position and served as the initial justification for criminalizing marijuana smoking.

The American Medical Association (AMA) represented the lone voice against marijuana prohibition before Congress. AMA Legislative Counsel Dr. William C. Woodward testified, "There is no evidence" that marijuana is a dangerous drug. Woodward challenged the propriety of passing legislation based only on newspaper accounts and questioned why no data from the Bureau of Prisons or the Children's Bureau supported the FBN's position. He further argued that the legislation would severely compromise a physician's ability to utilize marijuana's therapeutic potential.

Surprisingly, the committee took little interest in Woodward's testimony and told the physician, "If you want to advise us on legislation, you ought to come here with some constructive proposals . . . rather than trying to throw obstacles in the way of something that the federal government is trying to do."

After just one hearing, the Ways and Means Committee approved the "Marihuana Tax Act." The House of Representatives followed suit on August 20 after engaging in only 90 seconds of debate.

During this abbreviated floor "discussion," only two questions were asked. First, a member of Congress from upstate New York asked Speaker Sam Rayburn to summarize the purpose of the bill. Rayburn replied, "I don't know. It has something to do with a thing called marijuana. I think it is a narcotic of some kind." The same representative then asked, "Mr. Speaker, does the American Medical Association support the bill?" Falsely, a member of the Ways and Means Committee replied, "Their Doctor Wharton (sic) gave this measure his full support . . . [as well as] the approval [of] the American Medical Association." Following this brief exchange of inaccurate information, the House approved the federal prohibition of marijuana without a recorded vote.

Doughton's bill sailed though the Senate with the same ease. The Senate held one brief hearing on the bill before overwhelmingly approving the measure. President Franklin Roosevelt promptly signed the legislation into law on August 2, 1937. The "Marihuana Tax Act" took effect on October 1, 1937.

Thus began the criminal prohibition of marijuana that remains in place today. It was surely not a thoughtful or considered process that led to the federal prohibition of marijuana, and that tradition persists today when marijuana policy is occasionally revisited.

Marijuana prohibition: a costly failure

Current marijuana policy is a dismal and costly failure. It wastes untold billions of dollars in law enforcement resources, and needlessly wrecks the lives and careers of millions of our citizens. Yet marijuana remains the recreational drug of choice for millions of Americans.

Congress needs to move beyond the "reefer madness" phase of our marijuana policy, where elected officials attempt to frighten Americans into supporting the status quo by exaggerating marijuana's potential dangers. This is an issue about which most members of Congress are simply out of touch with their constituents, who know the difference between marijuana and more dangerous drugs, and who oppose spending $25,000 a year to jail an otherwise law-abiding marijuana smoker.

In fact, if marijuana smoking were dangerous, we would certainly know it; a significant segment of our population currently smokes marijuana recreationally, and there would be epidemiological evidence of harm among real people. No such evidence exists, despite millions of people who have smoked marijuana for years. So while we do need to fund more research on marijuana, especially research regarding medical uses—which, by the way, has been delayed by the federal government for years—we certainly know marijuana is relatively safe when used responsibly by adults.

It's time for Congress to let go of Reefer Madness, to end the crusade against marijuana and marijuana smokers, and to begin to deal with marijuana policy in a rational manner. The debate over marijuana policy in this Congress needs to be expanded beyond the current parameters to include consideration of (1) decriminalizing the marijuana smoker and (2) legalizing and regulating the sale of marijuana to eliminate the black market.

Arresting and jailing responsible marijuana smokers is a misapplication of the criminal sanction which undermines respect for the law in general.

(a) Millions of mainstream Americans have smoked marijuana. It is time to put to rest the myth that smoking marijuana is a fringe or deviant activity engaged in only by those on the margins of American society. In reality, marijuana smoking is extremely common and marijuana is the recreational drug of choice for millions of mainstream, middle class Americans. Government's surveys indicate more than 70 million Americans have smoked marijuana at some point in their lives, and that 18–20 million have smoked during the last year. Marijuana is the third most popular recreational drug of choice for Americans, exceeded only by alcohol and tobacco in popularity.

A national survey of voters conducted by the American Civil Liberties Union (ACLU) found that 32%—one third of the voting adults in the country—acknowledged having smoked marijuana at some point in their lives. Many successful business and professional leaders, including many state and federal elected officials from both political parties, admit they used marijuana. It is time to reflect that reality in our state and federal legislation, and stop acting as if marijuana smokers are part of the crime problem. They are not, and it is absurd to continue spending limited law enforcement resources arresting them.

Like most Americans, the vast majority of these millions of marijuana smokers are otherwise law-abiding citizens who work hard, raise families and contribute to their communities; they are indistinguishable from their non-smoking peers, except for their use of marijuana. They are not part of the crime problem and should not be treated like criminals. Arresting and jailing responsible marijuana smokers is a misapplication of the criminal sanction which undermines respect for the law in general.

Congress needs to acknowledge this constituency exists, and stop legislating as if marijuana smokers were dangerous people who need to be locked up. Marijuana smokers are simply average Americans.

(b) Marijuana arrests have skyrocketed. Current enforcement policies seem focused on arresting marijuana smokers. The FBI reports that police arrested 695,000 Americans, the highest number ever recorded, on marijuana charges in 1997 (the latest year for which data are available), and more than 3.7 million Americans this decade; *83% of these arrests were for simple possession, not sale.* Presently one American is arrested on marijuana charges every 45 seconds. Approximately 44 % of all drug arrests in this country are marijuana arrests. Despite criticism from some in Congress that President Bill Clinton was "soft" on drugs, annual data from the

Federal Bureau of Investigation's (FBI) Uniform Crime Report demonstrate that Clinton administration officials waged a more intensive war on marijuana smokers than any other presidency in history. Marijuana arrests more than doubled during President Clinton's time in office. This reality appears to conflict with statements by former White House Drug Czar Barry McCaffrey that America "can not arrest our way out of the drug problem."

Unfortunately, this renewed focus on marijuana smokers represents a shift away from enforcement against more dangerous drugs such as cocaine and heroin. Specifically, marijuana arrests have more than doubled during the 1990s while the percentage of arrests for the sale of cocaine and heroin have fallen 51%. Drug arrests have increased 31% in the last decade, and the increase in marijuana arrests accounts for most of that increase.

(c) Marijuana penalties cause enormous harm. Marijuana penalties vary nationwide, but most levy a heavy financial and social impact for the hundreds of thousands of Americans who are arrested each year. In 42 states, possession of any amount of marijuana is punishable by incarceration and/or a significant fine. Many states also have laws automatically suspending the driver's license of an individual if they are convicted of any marijuana offense, even if the offense was not driving related.

Penalties for marijuana cultivation and/or sale also vary from state to state. Ten states have maximum sentences of five years or less and eleven states have a maximum penalty of thirty years or more. Some states punish those who cultivate marijuana solely for personal use as severely as large scale traffickers. For instance, medical marijuana user William Foster of Oklahoma was sentenced to 93 years in jail in January 1997 for growing 10 medium-sized marijuana plants and 56 clones (cuttings from another plant planted in soil) in a 25-square-foot underground shelter. Foster maintains that he grew marijuana to alleviate the pain of rheumatoid arthritis. Unfortunately, Foster's plight is not an isolated event; marijuana laws in six states permit marijuana importers and traffickers to be sentenced to life in jail.

Congress needs to . . . stop legislating as if marijuana smokers were dangerous people who need to be locked up. Marijuana smokers are simply average Americans.

Federal laws prohibiting marijuana are also severe. Under federal law, possessing one marijuana cigarette or less is punishable by a fine of up to $10,000 and one year in prison, the same penalty as for possessing small amounts of heroin and cocaine. In one extreme case, attorney Edward Czuprynski of Michigan served 14 months in federal prison for possession of 1.6 grams of marijuana before a panel of federal appellate judges reviewed his case and demanded his immediate release. Cultivation of 100 marijuana plants or more carries a mandatory prison term of five years. Large scale marijuana cultivators and traffickers may be sentenced to death.

Federal laws also deny entitlements to marijuana smokers. Under legislation signed into law in 1996 states may deny cash aid (e.g., welfare, etc.) and food stamps to anyone convicted of felony drug charges. For marijuana smokers, this includes most convictions for cultivation and sale, even for small amounts and nonprofit transfers. More recently, Congress passed amendments in 1998 to the Higher Education Act which deny federal financial aid to any student with any drug conviction, even for a single marijuana cigarette. No other class of offense, including violent offenses, predatory offenses or alcohol-related offenses, carries automatic denial of federal financial aid eligibility. While substance abuse among our young people is a cause for concern, closing the doors of our colleges and universities, making it more difficult for at-risk young people to succeed, is not an appropriate response to a college student with a minor marijuana conviction.

Whether one smokes marijuana or drinks alcohol to relax is simply not an appropriate area of concern for the government.

Even those who avoid incarceration are subject to an array of punishments that may include submitting to random drug tests, probation, paying for mandatory drug counseling, loss of an occupational license, expensive legal fees, lost wages due to absence from work, loss of child custody, loss of federal benefits, and removal from public housing. In some states, police will notify the employer of people who are arrested, which frequently results in the loss of employment.

In addition, under both state and federal law, mere investigation for a marijuana offense can result in the forfeiture of property, including cash, cars, boats, land, business equipment, and houses. The owner does not have to be found guilty or even formally charged with any crime for the seizure to occur; 80% of those whose property is seized are never charged with a crime. Law enforcement can target suspected marijuana offenders for the purpose of seizing their property, sometimes with tragic results. For example, millionaire rancher Donald Scott was shot and killed by law enforcement officials in 1992 at his Malibu estate in a botched raid. Law enforcement failed to find any marijuana plants growing on his property and later conceded that their primary motivation for investigating Scott was to eventually seize his land.

State and federal marijuana laws also have a disparate racial impact on ethnic minorities. While blacks and Hispanics make up only 20 percent of the marijuana smokers in the U.S., they comprised 58 percent of the marijuana offenders sentenced under federal law in 1995. State arrest and incarceration rates paint a similar portrait. For example, in Illinois, 57 percent of those sent to prison for marijuana in 1995 were black or Hispanic. In California, 49 percent of those arrested for marijuana offenses in 1994 were black or Hispanic. And in New York state, 71 percent of those arrested for misdemeanor marijuana charges in 1995 were nonwhite.

Arresting and jailing otherwise law-abiding citizens who smoke marijuana is a wasteful and incredibly destructive policy. It wastes valuable law enforcement resources that should be focused on violent and serious crime; it invites government into areas of our private lives that are inappropriate; and it frequently destroys the lives, careers and families of genuinely good citizens. It is time to end marijuana prohibition.

Decriminalization is a commonsense option

In 1972, a blue-ribbon panel of experts appointed by President Richard Nixon and led by former Pennsylvania Governor Raymond Shafer concluded that marijuana prohibition posed significantly greater harm to the user than the use of marijuana itself. The National Commission on Marijuana and Drug Abuse recommended that state and federal laws be changed to remove criminal penalties for possession of marijuana for personal use and for the casual distribution of small amounts of marijuana. The report served as the basis for decriminalization bills adopted legislatively in 11 states during the 1970s.

A number of other prestigious governmental commissions have examined this issue over the last 25 years, and virtually all have reached the same conclusion: the purported dangers of marijuana smoking have been greatly overblown and the private use of marijuana by adults should not be a criminal matter. What former President Jimmy Carter said in a message to Congress in 1977, citing a key finding of the Marijuana Commission, is equally true today: "Penalties against drug use should not be more damaging to an individual than the use of the drug itself. Nowhere is this more clear than in the laws against possession of marijuana in private for personal use."

(a) Favorable experience with decriminalization in the U.S. Led by Oregon in 1973, 11 states adopted policies during the 1970s that removed criminal penalties for minor marijuana possession offenses and substituted a small civil fine enforced with a citation instead of an arrest. Today, approximately 30% of the population of this country live under some type of marijuana decriminalization law, and their experience has been favorable. The only U.S. federal study ever to compare marijuana use patterns among decriminalized states and those that have not found, "Decriminalization has had virtually no effect on either marijuana use or on related attitudes about marijuana use among young people." Dozens of privately commissioned follow up studies from the U.S. and abroad confirm this fact.

Decriminalization laws are popular with the voters, as evidenced by a 1998 state-wide vote in Oregon in which Oregonians voted 2 to 1 to reject a proposal, earlier adopted by their legislature, that would have reimposed criminal penalties for marijuana smokers. Oregonians clearly wanted to retain the decriminalization law that had worked well for nearly 30 years.

Since the Shafer Commission reported their findings to Congress in 1972 advocating marijuana decriminalization, over ten million Americans have been arrested on marijuana charges. Marijuana prohibition is a failed public policy that is out of touch with today's social reality and inflicts devastating harm on millions of citizens.

It is time we adopted a marijuana policy that recognizes a distinction between use and abuse, and reflects the importance most Americans place on the right of the individual to be free from the overreaching power of government. Most would agree that the government has no business knowing what books we read, the subject of our telephone conversations, or how we conduct ourselves in the bedroom. Similarly, whether one smokes marijuana or drinks alcohol to relax is simply not an appropriate area of concern for the government.

By stubbornly defining all marijuana smoking as criminal, including that which involves adults smoking in the privacy of their home, government is wasting police and prosecutorial resources, clogging courts, filling costly and scarce jail and prison space, and needlessly wrecking the lives and careers of genuinely good citizens.

It is time that Congress acknowledge what millions of Americans know to be true: there is nothing wrong with the responsible use of marijuana by adults and it should be of no interest or concern to the government.

In the final analysis, this debate is only incidentally about marijuana; it is really about personal freedom.

9

Marijuana Use Should Not Be Decriminalized

Damon Linker

Damon Linker is the associate editor of First Things, *a monthly journal published by the Institute on Religion and Public Life.*

The use of marijuana should not be decriminalized. While it is true that people cannot overdose on marijuana, legalization would make it widely available, which in turn would make it more difficult to prevent drug use among youth. Moreover, the pleasure of smoking marijuana differs from the pleasure of using alcohol or tobacco. Marijuana induces a euphoria that would otherwise occur only after the accomplishment of a virtuous and noble endeavor, such as artistic creation or religious devotion. When this euphoria fades, users are left with an empty feeling and a desire for another high. The unearned and artificially induced feelings of elation—coupled with the unproductiveness that pot users often exhibit—result in a spiritual malaise that warrants the drug's illegal status.

I t is safe to say that at some point in the not-too-distant future, America will confront the question of whether or not to legalize the use and cultivation of marijuana. A recent poll shows that support for legalization has reached its highest level since the question was first asked thirty years ago, with 34 percent supporting a liberalization of policy. Among political elites there is a growing consensus that the harsh penalties imposed on those who grow, use, and sell marijuana are disproportionate to its harmful effects. Even among conservatives, opinion seems to be shifting. Whether the change should be welcomed is another matter.

In an essay for *National Review*, Richard Lowry raises the question of whether marijuana is truly harmful—and he concludes that it isn't, or at least that it is significantly less so than any number of other drugs that are currently legal. Marijuana, he argues, "should be categorized somewhere between alcohol and tobacco on the one hand, and caffeine on the other." As evidence, he first points out that whereas "alcohol and tobacco kill hundreds of thousands of people a year," there is "no such thing as a lethal overdose of marijuana."

While this is certainly true, it is also the case that, strictly speaking, there is no such thing as a "lethal overdose" of tobacco. To the extent that tobacco causes deaths, it does so through the cumulative effects of smoking tobacco-filled cigarettes, cigars, and pipes. Unless Lowry intends to deny that most marijuana users get high through smoking it and that they usually do so without the filters commonly attached to cigarettes, one must assume that marijuana is at least as lethal as tobacco. As for alcohol, while it, unlike marijuana, can cause death when taken in extremely large doses, the same could also be said for such legal substances as aspirin. That it is possible for a drug to be taken in lethal quantities is, then, insufficient to determine whether it is harmful enough to be outlawed.

Much more potent is Lowry's argument against the conventional wisdom that pot is a "gateway drug" to such "harder" substances as LSD, cocaine, methamphetamine, and heroin. Reversing accepted assumptions, Lowry denies both that kids who use marijuana go on to experiment with stronger drugs and that those who do so are led to this behavior by the marijuana itself. As he points out, just "because a cocaine addict used marijuana first doesn't mean he is on cocaine because he smoked marijuana." To argue in this way is, he claims, to confuse "temporality with causality." It is more likely that children who experiment with drugs of all kinds do so because of a preexisting behavioral problem. It's thus "the kid, not the substance, who is the problem."

The danger of widely available drugs

Like the National Rifle Association's effective campaign to persuade the country that "guns don't kill people, people kill people," Lowry's argument contains much truth. Of course a troubled child is more likely to try drugs than one with a firm sense of right and wrong. But that's far from being the end of the story. Just as a would-be murderer can usually do far more harm with a gun than he could with a less potent weapon, so a child in danger of losing his way can do more damage to himself when drugs are widely available for his use, as they surely would be if they were legalized.

> *A child in danger of losing his way can do more damage to himself when drugs are widely available for his use, as they surely would be if they were legalized.*

And then there is the question of education. The behavioral problems that Lowry points to as the true cause of drug abuse do not arise in a vacuum. They come about largely from a failure of moral education—by schools, but much more so by parents. As it is, the law provides a small but significant amount of support for parents in their efforts to steer their kids away from drugs. Libertarians may argue that legalization would not undermine those efforts—that it would merely leave it up to individuals to decide for themselves—but as opponents of the unlimited abortion license are well aware, legal neutrality is often far from neutral. When we outlaw some actions (like murder) and permit others (like abortion) we make a crucially important distinction. We teach that the former are unambiguously wrong and that the latter are not. To legalize marijuana is thus to weaken the position of parents who wish to steel their children against the temptation of drug-taking.

Marijuana . . . provides its users with a means to enjoy the rewards of excellence without possessing it themselves.

But Lowry nevertheless has a point. If it is true that few users of marijuana become users of other drugs, then the rationale for keeping pot illegal has indeed been undermined. Add to this the scientifically established fact that, unlike alcohol, nicotine, and cocaine, marijuana is not physically addictive, and we cannot help but wonder if we should conclude, with Lowry, that marijuana is relatively harmless, and thus that punishing people for using it is "outrageously disproportionate."

Distinguishing among kinds of pleasure

In two columns for the *New Republic*, Andrew Sullivan goes beyond Lowry's position to declare flatly that "the illegal thing in pot is not THC [its active ingredient]; it's pleasure." And this, he claims, is absurd. In a country that increasingly medicates itself with pharmaceuticals, which, like pot, induce pleasure by manipulating chemicals already present in the human body, criminalizing the use and cultivation of marijuana appears to be completely arbitrary. In fact, according to Sullivan, it is only a "residual cultural puritanism" that stands in the way of allowing Americans to pursue "enjoyment" however they wish. "It is bizarre," he writes, "that, in a country founded in part on the pursuit of happiness, we should now be expending so many resources on incarcerating and terrorizing so many people simply because they are doing what their Constitution promised." Sure, he admits, "pleasure isn't the same thing as happiness." But "the responsible, adult enjoyment of . . . pleasure . . . is surely part of it."

The argument is a powerful one. If, in the end, the dispute about legalizing marijuana can be reduced to a conflict between those who support pleasure and those who oppose it, then the prohibitionists have already lost the argument. The Puritans simply won't be winning any elections in twenty-first century America. Nevertheless, we have reason to think that a case against legalization can be based on a less exacting distinction. That is, we can insist on distinguishing among kinds of pleasure, something that, common sense notwithstanding, Lowry and Sullivan each steadfastly refuse to do.

While most people believe that pleasure is a good thing, they also categorize and rank its different types. Some pleasures are subtle, others are intense. Some are best experienced alone, others can be enjoyed only in community. Some are base, others noble. Some are purely physical, while others are inextricably bound up with our higher powers. And then there are those most fulfilling pleasures—the ones that follow from the completion of the highest human endeavors. The late author and political science professor Allan Bloom noted the occasions that tend to elicit such feelings: "victory in a just war, consummated love, artistic creation, religious devotion, and the discovery of truth."

The pleasure of smoking marijuana differs from the kind of pleasure that accompanies smoking a fine cigar or sipping a well-brewed cup of coffee, and more pertinently, it also differs from the pleasure of mild drunkenness. Whereas alcohol primarily diminishes one's inhibitions and clarity of thought, marijuana inspires a euphoria that resembles nothing so much as the pleasure that normally arises only in response to the accomplishment of the noblest human deeds. Marijuana, like the designer drug Ecstasy, whose legalization Sullivan also, revealingly, supports, provides its users with a means to enjoy the rewards of excellence without possessing it themselves. Bloom again: "Without effort, without talent, without virtue, without exercise of the faculties, anyone and everyone is accorded the equal right to the enjoyment of their fruits."

A pathology of the soul

A country that consumes ever-greater doses of mood-altering prescription drugs might not deem this to be a significant problem, but it should. The danger is not merely that seeking happiness through pharmacology cuts us off from the world as it truly is. It is also that the very attempt to reach happiness in such a way must ultimately fail. While Sullivan is right to remark on the distinction between pleasure and happiness, he neglects to follow up on his insight—to think through what it is that separates them. If he had done so, he would have noted that, whereas pleasure involves enjoying something good, happiness arises only when we judge ourselves worthy of enjoying it.

This is why such actions as a just military victory can produce happiness, while inhaling marijuana smoke, however pleasurable, can lead only to an ersatz satisfaction—because it involves nothing praiseworthy. Thus it is that, after its effects have worn off, marijuana leaves its users with little more than a feeling of emptiness and a craving for another high to fill it. Hence also the unproductive stupor into which "potheads" frequently fall.

Lowry and Sullivan may be right to claim that marijuana does not lead to physical harm. But it does produce a pathology of the soul. And given the many pathogens that already pollute our culture—as well as our society's salutary prejudice against marijuana—that is reason enough to resist the efforts of some to remove the legal obstacles to getting high.

10

Medical Marijuana Should Be Legalized

Marijuana Policy Project

The Marijuana Policy Project is an educational and lobbying organization that works to reform marijuana laws at the federal level.

Marijuana is a safe medicine that is useful in the symptomatic treatment of several ailments, including AIDS, epilepsy, glaucoma, cancer, and multiple sclerosis. However, marijuana is still classified as a Schedule I drug, meaning that it is officially defined as addictive and of no medicinal value. Although state legislatures can elect to remove state-level prohibitions on the use of medical marijuana, they remain restricted in their legalization efforts because of the federal government's overriding marijuana criminalization laws. The U.S. Congress should revise federal laws to allow seriously ill people access to therapeutic cannabis.

For thousands of years, marijuana has been used to treat a wide variety of ailments. Until 1937, marijuana (*Cannabis sativa L.*) was legal in the United States for all purposes. Presently, federal law allows only seven (7) Americans to use marijuana as a medicine.

On March 17, 1999, the National Academy of Sciences' Institute of Medicine (IOM) concluded that "there are some limited circumstances in which we recommend smoking marijuana for medical uses." The IOM report released that day was the result of two years of research that was funded by the White House drug policy office, which comprised a meta-analysis of all existing data on marijuana's therapeutic uses. *Please see www.mpp.org/science.html.*

Medicinal value

Marijuana is one of the safest therapeutically active substances known. No one has ever died from an overdose, and it has a wide variety of therapeutic applications:
  • Relief from nausea and increase of appetite;

- Reduction of intraocular ("within the eye") pressure;
- Reduction of muscle spasms;
- Relief from chronic pain.

Marijuana is frequently beneficial in the treatment of the following conditions:

- *AIDS.* Marijuana can reduce the nausea, vomiting, and loss of appetite caused by the ailment itself and by various AIDS medications.
- *Glaucoma.* Marijuana can reduce intraocular pressure, thereby alleviating the pain and slowing—and sometimes stopping—the progress of the condition. (Glaucoma is the leading cause of blindness in the United States. It damages vision by increasing eye pressure over time.)
- *Cancer.* Marijuana can stimulate the appetite and alleviate nausea and vomiting, which are common side effects of chemotherapy treatment.
- *Multiple Sclerosis.* Marijuana can limit the muscle pain and spasticity caused by the disease, as well as relieving tremor and unsteadiness of gait. (Multiple sclerosis is the leading cause of neurological disability among young and middle-aged adults in the United States.)
- *Epilepsy.* Marijuana can prevent epileptic seizures in some patients.
- *Chronic Pain.* Marijuana can alleviate the chronic, often debilitating pain caused by myriad disorders and injuries.

Marijuana is useful for treating arthritis, migraine, menstrual cramps, alcohol and opiate addiction, and depression.

Each of these applications has been deemed legitimate by at least one court, legislature, and/or government agency in the United States.

Many patients also report that marijuana is useful for treating arthritis, migraine, menstrual cramps, alcohol and opiate addiction, and depression and other debilitating mood disorders.

Marijuana could be helpful for millions of patients in the United States. Nevertheless, other than for the *seven* people with special permission from the federal government, medical marijuana remains illegal!

People currently suffering from any of the conditions mentioned above, for whom the legal medical options have proven unsafe or ineffective, have two options:

1. Continue to suffer from the ailment itself; or
2. Illegally obtain marijuana—and risk suffering consequences such as:
   - an insufficient supply due to the prohibition-inflated price or scarcity;
   - impure, contaminated, or chemically adulterated marijuana;
   - arrests, fines, court costs, property forfeiture, incarceration, probation, and criminal records.

Marijuana prohibition

Prior to 1937, at least 27 medicines containing marijuana were legally available in the United States. Many were made by well-known pharmaceutical firms that still exist today, such as Squibb (now Bristol-Myers

Squibb) and Eli Lilly. The Marijuana Tax Act of 1937 federally prohibited marijuana. Dr. William C. Woodward of the American Medical Association opposed the Act, testifying that prohibition would ultimately prevent the medicinal uses of marijuana.

The Controlled Substances Act of 1970 placed all illicit and prescription drugs into five "schedules" (categories). *Marijuana was placed in Schedule I, defining it as having a high potential for abuse, no currently accepted medicinal use in treatment in the United States, and a lack of accepted safety for use under medical supervision.*

Congress [should] change federal law so that seriously ill people nationwide can use medical marijuana without fear of arrest and imprisonment.

This definition simply does not apply to marijuana. Of course, at the time of the Controlled Substances Act, marijuana had been prohibited for more than three decades. Its medicinal uses forgotten, marijuana was considered a dangerous and addictive narcotic.

A substantial increase in the number of recreational users in the 1970s contributed to the rediscovery of marijuana's medicinal uses:

- Many scientists studied the health effects of marijuana and inadvertently discovered marijuana's astonishing medicinal history in the process.
- Many who used marijuana recreationally also suffered from diseases for which marijuana is beneficial. By fluke, they discovered its therapeutic usefulness.

As the word spread, more and more patients started self-medicating with marijuana. However, marijuana's Schedule I status bars doctors from prescribing it and severely curtails research.

In 1972, a petition was submitted to the Bureau of Narcotics and Dangerous Drugs—now the Drug Enforcement Administration (DEA)—to reschedule marijuana to make it available by prescription.

After 16 years of court battles, the DEA's chief administrative law judge, Francis L. Young, ruled:

> Marijuana, in its natural form, is one of the safest therapeutically active substances known. . . .
>
> . . . [T]he provisions of the [Controlled Substances] Act permit and require the transfer of marijuana from Schedule I to Schedule II.
>
> It would be unreasonable, arbitrary and capricious for DEA to continue to stand between those sufferers and the benefits of this substance. . . .
>
> (September 6, 1988)

Marijuana's placement in Schedule II would enable doctors to prescribe it to their patients. *But top DEA bureaucrats rejected Judge Young's ruling and refused to reschedule marijuana.* Two appeals later, petitioners experienced their first defeat in the 22-year-old lawsuit. On February 18,

1994, the U.S. Court of Appeals (D.C. Circuit) ruled that the DEA is allowed to reject its judge's ruling and set its own criteria—enabling the DEA to keep marijuana in Schedule I.

However, Congress still has the power to reschedule marijuana via legislation, regardless of the DEA's wishes.

Temporary compassion

In 1975, Robert Randall, who suffered from glaucoma, was arrested for cultivating his own marijuana. He won his case by using the "medical necessity defense," forcing the government to find a way to provide him with his medicine. As a result, the Investigational New Drug (IND) compassionate access program was established, enabling some patients to receive marijuana from the government.

The program was grossly inadequate at helping the potentially millions of people who need medical marijuana:

- Most patients would never consider the idea that an illegal drug might be their best medicine;
- Most patients fortunate enough to discover marijuana's medicinal value did not discover the IND program;
- Most of those who did learn of the program could not find doctors willing to take on the arduous task of enrolling in and working through the IND program.

In 1992, in response to a flood of new applications from AIDS patients, the George Bush administration closed the program to all new applicants. On December 1, 1999, the Bill Clinton administration restated that the IND program would not be reopened. Consequently, the IND program remains in operation only for the seven surviving previously approved patients.

Public opinion

There is tremendous public support for ending the prohibition of medical marijuana:

- Since 1996, a majority of voters in Alaska, California, Colorado, the District of Columbia, Maine, Nevada, Oregon, and Washington state have voted in favor of ballot initiatives to remove criminal penalties for seriously ill people who grow or possess medical marijuana. Recent polls have shown that public approval of these laws has increased since they went into effect.
- A 1990 scientific survey of oncologists (cancer specialists) found that 54% of those with an opinion favored the controlled medical availability of marijuana and 44% had already broken the law by suggesting at least once that a patient obtain marijuana illegally.
- A Pew Research poll conducted February 14–19, 2001, found that 73% of American adults supported permitting doctors to prescribe marijuana for their patients. Over the last decade, polls have consistently shown between 60% and 80% support for legal access to medical marijuana.

The federal government has no legal authority to prevent state governments from changing their laws to remove state-level criminal penalties for medical marijuana use. Indeed, Hawaii enacted a medical marijuana law via its state legislature in June 2000. State legislatures have the authority and moral responsibility to change state law to:

- exempt seriously ill patients from state-level prosecution for medical marijuana possession and cultivation; and
- exempt doctors who recommend medical marijuana from prosecution or the denial of any right or privilege.

Even within the confines of federal law, states can enact reforms that have the practical effect of removing the fear of patients being arrested and prosecuted under state law—as well as the symbolic effect of pushing the federal government to allow doctors to prescribe marijuana.

State governments that want to allow marijuana to be sold in pharmacies have been stymied by the federal government's overriding prohibition of marijuana.

Patients' efforts to bring change through the federal courts have made little progress, as the courts tend to defer to the DEA, which is aggressively working to keep marijuana illegal.

Efforts to obtain FDA approval of marijuana are similarly stalled. Though some small-scale studies of marijuana are now underway, the National Institute on Drug Abuse—the only legal source of marijuana for clinical research in the U.S.—has consistently made it difficult (and often nearly impossible) for researchers to obtain marijuana for their studies. Under the present circumstances, it is virtually impossible to do the sort of large-scale and extremely costly trials required for FDA approval.

In the meantime, patients continue to suffer. *Congress has the power and the responsibility to change federal law so that seriously ill people nationwide can use medical marijuana without fear of arrest and imprisonment.*

11

Medical Marijuana Should Not Be Legalized

Colin Lowry

Colin Lowry writes for 21st Century, *a quarterly science journal.*

Marijuana is much less effective as a medicine than recent media reports indicate. According to a 1999 study conducted by the Institute of Medicine, marijuana smoke actually harms the lungs, suppresses the immune system, and causes brain damage. While marijuana has often been touted as a helpful remedy for nausea in chemotherapy patients, it is actually less effective than many other legally available antinausea drugs. Furthermore, marijuana is not a useful treatment for glaucoma or pain. The attempt to redefine this damaging and addictive drug as medicine is simply pro-drug propaganda.

In the past few years, ballot initiatives permitting the medical use of marijuana, supposedly to treat chronically ill patients, have been approved in several states. These initiatives have been funded by the notorious international speculator George Soros, as a "Trojan Horse" for the legalization of illicit drugs. In response to this campaign, the Institute of Medicine (IOM) was commissioned to conduct a review of the scientific evidence "to assess the potential health benefits and risks of marijuana and its constituent cannabinoids," by the White House Office of National Drug Control Policy in January 1997.

The IOM report, released on March 17, 1999, reviews the biological effects of marijuana, documenting the damage it does to the brain's cognitive functions and motor coordination, its suppression of immune system function, and its damage to the reproductive system.

The report also compares the effectiveness of marijuana to other drugs already in use to treat pain and nausea, finding it much less effective than currently prescribed drugs. In its conclusions, the IOM recommended against the use of smoked marijuana, citing the damage done by the tar and carcinogens to the lungs of users. It also concludes that the family of compounds known as cannabinoids, found in marijuana, may be useful for future drug development—the only conclusion to be played up, and distorted, by the media.

Damaging effects of cannabinoids

The substance of the IOM report documents the damaging effects of cannabinoids.

There are about 60 chemicals known as cannabinoids found in marijuana, of which delta-9-tetrahydrocannabinol, known as THC, is the most abundant of the psychoactive compounds. THC produces most of its effects in the brain and body by binding to specific receptors on the cell surface of neurons, or other cell types. One type of cannabinoid receptor was first found in the brain in 1990; a second type was found outside the brain in 1993. In 1992, a natural compound produced by the brain, called anandamide, was found to bind to the cannabinoid receptors, but its function remains mostly unknown. By also binding to these receptors, THC is interfering in a natural chemical signal pathway in the brain.

The most consistent damage produced by chronic THC administration is loss of short-term memory. The area of the brain involved in short-term memory, and its transfer into long-term memory, is the hippocampus, which has a high concentration of cannabinoid receptors. Chronic marijuana users become tolerant of THC, and therefore have to smoke more and more to get the same "high." This causes permanent damage to the hippocampus, and may result in the inability to transfer information from short-term memory into long-term memory, a condition associated with Alzheimer's disease.

[The] THC from marijuana reduces the resistance to infection.

Studies of performance requiring auditory attention in people who have smoked only one marijuana cigarette show impaired performance, and this is associated with a substantial decrease in blood flow to the temporal lobe of the brain.

Cannabinoids also affect spatial memory, balance, and coordination. The cerebellum is largely responsible for coordinating motor control of the body, and this brain region also has a high concentration of cannabinoid receptors. A study of experienced airplane pilots showed that even 24 hours after the smoking of a single marijuana cigarette, their performance on flight-simulator tests was impaired.

In addition, the regulation of hormones in the brain is altered by cannabinoids. Studies have shown that chronic THC administration in rats induces aging-like degenerative changes, which resemble the effects of stress exposure and elevated corticosteroid secretion.

Immunosuppression

One of the most serious consequences of the use of marijuana as a drug is the suppression of the immune system's function. Lymphocytes, including T-cells, which are responsible for fighting infection, are inhibited from proliferating by THC. B-cells, which produce antibodies that bind to foreign pathogens, are often inhibited from becoming active by THC, and even at very low doses, antibody production is reduced. THC also interferes with signals in the immune system that are mediated by cytokines. Studies in mice have shown that THC suppresses the cytokines that modulate the response to infection, and that the overall cytokine profile produced is abnormal.

Another detrimental effect is that THC from marijuana reduces the resistance to infection. In experiments with mice given THC, and then infected with sublethal doses of pneumonia-causing bacteria, most of these mice failed to fight the infection, and died of septic shock. However, control mice that were not exposed to THC fought off the infection, and became immune to repeated challenge by the bacteria.

Ludicrous claims

Considering these dangerous consequences to human health from marijuana use, it is ludicrous to propose its use as a medicine. For example: One of the most ballyhooed proposed uses of marijuana is to treat nausea and weight loss experienced by AIDS patients. THC is not very effective at treating nausea, and the doses required for a modest effect are strongly hallucinogenic. Further, 90 percent of these AIDS patients are treated successfully with drugs already available. For the approximately 10 percent of AIDS patients who do not respond to standard treatments, synthetic THC, known as Marinol, can be legally prescribed in the United States.

However, THC is an immunosuppressant, so why would anyone want to give an AIDS patient, whose immune system is already gravely impaired, a drug that would decrease his or her resistance to infection?

Another of the proposed uses touted for marijuana is to treat nausea in cancer patients undergoing chemotherapy. The IOM report found that in clinical trials, THC provided only moderate control of nausea in 13 percent of the patients, as compared to drugs already available, which achieved complete control of nausea in almost 50 percent of the patients.

A profile of members of "medical use" cannabis buyers' clubs in California is included in the IOM report. Most of these "medical" users have used "recreational" drugs in the past, and more than 50 percent of these marijuana smokers tested positive for cocaine or amphetamines.

The IOM report also shot down the anecdotal evidence that marijuana is effective at treating glaucoma. In fact, marijuana was found to be *ineffective* at lowering the pressure in the eye of glaucoma patients over a period of time longer than a few hours. The report also found marijuana to be only mildly capable of treating pain, being slightly less effective than codeine.

Although the report's conclusions eliminated smoked marijuana as effective at treating symptoms of diseases such as multiple sclerosis and Parkinson's disease, it did not adequately emphasize marijuana's damage to the cognitive functions of the brain. What the IOM report should have said, is that attempts to portray this damaging drug as a medicine, are nothing but propaganda for drug legalization.

12

States Should Be Allowed to Construct Their Own Marijuana Laws

James P. Pinkerton

James P. Pinkerton is a columnist for Newsday *in New York City.*

States should be allowed to frame their own policies on marijuana use. Currently, federal law bars states from allowing the distribution of medical marijuana—even when the state population elects to permit it. But laws concerning many other issues—including gun control, school choice, tax cuts, and gay civil unions—are decided at the state level by ballots and legislatures, and marijuana laws should be too.

The Supreme Court's decision in August 2000 barring the distribution of medical marijuana in California is a reminder to the political left that the federal government—specifically, the federal judiciary—is not its automatic ally. The political right, of course, has long seen the feds as foes, and so now maybe both ends of the spectrum will see that the real enemy is a one-size-fits-all approach to national governance.

"This is about more than just marijuana," Dennis Peron, a Bay Area medical marijuana activist, told *The Times*. "It's about the Supreme Court interfering with states' rights."

Whoa. "States' rights?" That's a blast from the past. In 1948, South Carolina's Strom Thurmond ran for president as a states' rights Democrat, denying that the federal government had any grounds to interfere with racial segregation in Dixie. With such precedents in mind, it's little wonder that when most Americans hear "states' rights," they hear code words for reaction.

A helpful new approach

But that's not the whole story. One can insist on minimum national standards for, say, civil rights, and still see the value of the 50 states having different prototypes for problem-solving. David Osborne, the godfather of the "reinventing government" movement, set the tone for a revival of state-by-state experimentation in his 1990 book, *Laboratories of Democracy: A New Breed of Governor Creates Models for National Growth.* Osborne highlighted the economic-development efforts of such up-and-comers as Bill Clinton, then the governor of Arkansas; it was Clinton himself who argued, during the 1992 campaign, that new ideas from outside the Beltway were needed to overcome the "brain-dead gridlock" of the capital.

In the '90s, the states enacted new approaches to issues all across the political spectrum, from term limits to gay and lesbian civil unions, from tax cuts to spending increases, from school choice to school uniforms, from gun control to "concealed carry" gun permits, from campaign finance reform to voting by mail, even by Internet. And the diverse beat goes on. At a time when many Americans, especially along the Mexican border, are worried about too many immigrants, Iowa, worried about having too few people, is calling itself an "immigration enterprise zone"; the land-locked Hawkeye State wants to be the Ellis Island of the prairie.

It may seem ironic that Clinton—the first product of the Swinging '60s to sit in the Oval Office, the erstwhile try-new-things governor—backs [former] national drug czar Barry R. McCaffrey as he seeks to squelch California's approach to the drug issue. In 1996, Golden State voters enacted Proposition 215, the Compassionate Use Act, authorizing nonprofit groups to distribute marijuana to doctor-certified medical patients.

Yet McCaffrey & Co. view such "cannabis clubs" as the thin edge of the wedge, as a tactic used by legalization advocates to bring marijuana into the mainstream. And at the Department of Justice's urging, the U.S. Supreme Court agreed, voting 7-1—including Clinton appointee Ruth Bader Ginsberg—to shut down medical marijuana distribution.

Coincidentally, as the Supreme Court issued its ruling, Clinton was on his way to Colombia, where the federal government is about to spend an additional $1.3 billion on an increasingly quagmirish drug war. And when President I-Didn't-Inhale comes back to the U.S., he'll be walking free, as the prisons bulge with 2 million inmates, the bulk of them there for drug-related offenses.

No doubt most Americans support Clinton's drug efforts. But not all do. And that's where the question of states' rights comes in. Should California have the option of going a different direction from the rest of the nation on drug policy? Is the national interest really served by imposing a toughest-common-denominator policy on the entire country? Today, Utah, with fewer than 2 million people, has more influence on national drug policy than California, with 30 million people. Why? Because Sen. Orrin Hatch (R-Utah), a drug hawk, chairs the Judiciary Committee, through which every federal judge must be confirmed.

It doesn't have to be this way. It's possible to imagine a decentralized system in which the states would be free, or at least freer, to go their own way on all manner of social policy—to the left, to the right, to wherever. Call it "states' rights," call it "federalism," or call it simply "diversity." By any name, it would smell sweet, because the real word for it is "freedom."

13

State-Level Marijuana Laws Could Undermine the National Stance Against Drugs

David F. Musto

David F. Musto is a professor at the Yale School of Medicine and author of The American Disease: Origins of Narcotic Control.

Marijuana policy should not be decided at the state level. The prohibition of dangerous drugs is an overriding national concern that requires federal-level decision making. While some states are attempting to legalize medical marijuana, there is no conclusive evidence proving that the drug is an effective medicine. If states such as California are allowed to repeal antimarijuana laws, it would weaken the nation's unified stance against drugs.

A re our federal marijuana laws unraveling? There is reason to think so. Early in the 20th century, each state had its own laws controlling habit-forming drugs, unaffected by federal statutes. In 1914, for example, it was legal in New York to be maintained on morphine, while in Massachusetts it was illegal for a physician to supply morphine to a habitual user.

After lengthy attempts to control morphine, heroin and cocaine, Congress in 1914 passed the Harrison Act, which imposed one rule on these drugs throughout the nation. The law was typical of Progressive Era legislation: A national problem that was being dealt with variously by the states was harmonized by one overriding federal law.

A similar patchwork pattern applied to marijuana in the 1920s when it first became a serious worry. Then in 1937, national control also was applied to marijuana. The Marihuana Tax Act made it illegal to buy, sell, barter, etc., marijuana anywhere in the United States unless you had purchased a marijuana tax stamp, and there were, for all practical purposes, no stamps to be bought. This held true until 1970, when the basis for the anti-marijuana law was shifted from the tax power of the federal government to interstate commerce powers, but the overriding control of marijuana continues to reside with the federal government.

California is pulling the nation toward a dismantling of a national consensus against marijuana.

Usually when a problem has been formulated into a national law, the several states accept this resolution; any alterations are argued in Congress.

Unraveling the national law

But there are exceptions. Passing welfare from the federal government to the states is a major shift in the locus of control. A similar trend toward unraveling what long ago had been knitted into national law may be occurring with control of dangerous drugs. Even the U.S. Supreme Court's decision in the year 2000 to prohibit sale of "medicinal marijuana" in Oakland, California, at least for the time being, may be just a skirmish in the devolution of drug control from Washington to the states. For example, the U.S. 9th Circuit Court of Appeals has taken the position that the "medical necessity" of marijuana outweighs the federal statute that makes marijuana illicit, an issue that may come before the Supreme Court this fall. [In 2001 the Supreme Court barred a medical-necessity exemption to the federal law criminalizing marijuana.]

If enough of the judiciary were to follow suit, we would have in effect the repeal of the anti-marijuana statute. We would be moving toward an earlier era of variegated state regulations.

The marijuana question raises two issues: the value of marijuana as a medicine, and the right to use marijuana for simple recreation. Some of us may believe that those who want to exercise their right to smoke for any reason use the medical marijuana issue to achieve adoption of laws that loosen controls at the state level. Still, an important question remains: Does cannabis have some characteristics that give it unique healing or comforting properties? We do not have a good answer to this. The claims for marijuana are often anecdotal, not scientifically established.

Coincidentally, the day the Supreme Court made its pronouncement regarding Oakland, the University of California announced that it was opening two centers, in San Francisco and San Diego, to study the health value of cannabis. Gen. Barry R. McCaffrey, [former] director of the White House Office of National Drug Control Policy, has said—and reasonably so—that if cannabis were proved to have medical benefits he would favor its use in a medically approved delivery system. Several years ago, the Food and Drug Administration approved a liquid form of cannabis' active ingredient, tetrahydrocannabinol, or THC, for physicians to prescribe, although it does not seem to have become a popular remedy.

Interestingly, the late Harry J. Anslinger, the legendary head of the federal Bureau of Narcotics and Dangerous Drugs from 1930 to 1962,

wanted to avoid a federal marijuana law: He urged the states to individu-
ally enact a uniform state narcotic act that included marijuana. He told
me in the early 1970s that he felt this way because the task of eradicating
marijuana was beyond his ability and also because he realized that he
would be given neither more money nor more agents when he was given
the task in 1937 of controlling marijuana.

If each state had a law, then each state could decide for itself how
much of its resources it wanted to devote to the control of pot, and federal authorities could concern themselves with just opiates and cocaine.

California was one of the Western states that clamored for a federal
anti-marijuana law in the 1930s. The perceived connection between Mexican immigrants and marijuana use lay behind some of the most insistent
demands for action, but there were also more reasoned concerns about
marijuana use, especially among youth.

Sixty-some years after pushing for the Marihuana Tax Act, California
is pulling the nation toward a dismantling of a national consensus
against marijuana.

Organizations to Contact

The editors have compiled the following list of organizations concerned with the issues debated in this book. The descriptions are derived from materials provided by the organizations. All have publications or information available for interested readers. The list was compiled on the date of publication of the present volume; the information provided here may change. Be aware that many organizations take several weeks or longer to respond to inquiries, so allow as much time as possible.

American Civil Liberties Union (ACLU)
125 Broad St., 18th Fl., New York, NY 10004-2400
(212) 549-2500 • fax: (212) 549-2646
e-mail: aclu@aclu.org • website: www.aclu.org

The ACLU is a national organization that works to defend Americans' civil rights guaranteed by the U.S. Constitution. It provides legal defense, research, and education. The ACLU opposes the criminal prohibition of marijuana and the civil liberties violations that result from it. Its publications include "Why Marijuana Reform Law Should Matter to You," and "Democracy Held Hostage: How Marijuana Made Bob Barr So Paranoid He Canceled an Election."

American Council for Drug Education (ACDE)
164 W. 74th St., New York, NY 10023
(800) 488-3784 • (212) 595-5810, ext. 7860 • fax: (212) 595-2553
e-mail: acde@phoenixhouse.org • website: www.acde.org

The American Council for Drug Education informs the public about the harmful effects of abusing drugs and alcohol. It gives the public access to scientifically based, compelling prevention programs and materials. ACDE has resources for parents, youth, educators, prevention professionals, employers, health care professionals, and other concerned community members who are working to help America's youth avoid the dangers of drug and alcohol abuse.

Canadian Foundation for Drug Policy (CFDP)
70 MacDonald St., Ottawa, ON K2P 1H6 CANADA
(613) 236-1027 • fax: (613) 238-2891
e-mail: eoscapel@cfdp.ca • website: www.cfdp.ca

Founded by several of Canada's leading drug policy specialists, CFDP examines the objectives and consequences of Canada's drug laws and policies, including laws concerning marijuana. When necessary, the foundation recommends alternatives that it believes would make Canada's drug policies more effective and humane. CFDP discusses drug policy issues with the Canadian government, media, and general public. It also disseminates educational materials and maintains a website with an archive of news articles, studies, and reports.

Drug Enforcement Administration (DEA)
Mailstop: AXS, 2401 Jefferson Davis Highway, Alexandria, VA 22301
(202) 307-1000
website: www.usdoj.gov/dea

The DEA is the federal agency charged with enforcing the nation's drug laws. The agency concentrates on stopping the smuggling and distribution of narcotics in the United States and abroad. It publishes the *Drug Enforcement Magazine* three times a year.

Drug Policy Alliance
925 15th St. NW, Washington, DC 20005
(202) 216-0035 • fax: (202) 216-0803
e-mail: dc@drugpolicy.org • website: www.dpf.org

The Drug Policy Alliance is a merging of the Lindesmith Center, formerly the leading drug policy reform institute in the United States, and the Drug Policy Foundation, a nonprofit organization that advocated sensible and humane drug policies. These two organizations joined in the year 2000 with the objective of building a national drug policy reform movement. The alliance works to broaden the public debate on drug policy and to promote realistic alternatives to the war on drugs based on science, compassion, public health, and human rights. It supports the legalization of marijuana for medical purposes. Reports available on its website include "Selling Pot: The Pitfalls of Marijuana Reform," and "Facts and Myths About Marijuana."

Family Research Council
801 G St. NW, Washington, DC 20001
(202) 393-2100 • order line: (800) 225-4008
website: www.frc.org

The council analyzes issues affecting the family and seeks to ensure that the interests of the traditional family are considered in the formulation of public policy. It lobbies legislatures and promotes public debate on issues concerning the family. The council publishes articles and position papers against the legalization of medicinal marijuana.

Marijuana Policy Project
PO Box 77492, Capitol Hill, Washington, DC 20013
(202) 462-5747 • fax: (202) 232-0442
e-mail: info@mpp.org • website: www.mpp.org

The Marijuana Policy Project develops and promotes policies to minimize the harm associated with marijuana. It is the only organization that is solely concerned with lobbying to reform the marijuana laws on the federal level. The project increases public awareness through speaking engagements, educational seminars, the mass media, and briefing papers. Its website contains an archive of recent news releases.

Multidisciplinary Association for Psychedelic Studies (MAPS)
2105 Robinson Ave., Sarasota, FL 34232
(941) 924-6277 • (888) 868-6277
e-mail: info@maps.org • website: www.maps.org

MAPS is a membership-based research and educational organization. It focuses on the development of beneficial, socially sanctioned uses of psychedelic drugs and marijuana. MAPS helps scientific researchers obtain governmental approval for, fund, conduct, and report on psychedelic research in human volunteers. It publishes the quarterly *MAPS Bulletin* as well as various reports and newsletters.

National Center on Addiction and Substance Abuse (CASA)
Columbia University
633 Third Ave., 19th Floor, New York, NY 10017-6706
(212) 841-5200 • fax: (212) 956-8020
website: www.casacolumbia.org

CASA is a private nonprofit organization that works to educate the public about the hazards of chemical dependency. The organization supports treatment as the best way to reduce chemical dependency. It produces publications describing the harmful effects of alcohol and drug addiction and effective ways to address the problem of substance abuse.

National Clearinghouse for Alcohol and Drug Information
11426-28 Rockville Pike, Suite 200, Rockville, MD 20052
(800) 729-6686
e-mail: webmaster@health.org • website: www.health.org

The clearinghouse distributes publications of the U.S. Department of Health and Human Services, the National Institute on Drug Abuse, and other federal agencies concerned with alcohol and drug abuse. Papers available through its website include "Prevention Alert: Did 'Sixties Parents' Hurt Their Kids?" and "10 Things Every Teen Should Know About Marijuana."

National Institute on Drug Abuse (NIDA)
National Institutes of Health
6001 Executive Blvd., Room 5213, Bethesda, MD 20892-9561
(301) 443-1124
e-mail: information@lists.nida.nih.gov • website: www.nida.nih.gov

NIDA supports and conducts research on drug abuse—including the yearly Monitoring the Future Survey—to improve addiction prevention, treatment, and policy efforts. It publishes the bimonthly *NIDA Notes* newsletter, the periodic *NIDA Capsules* fact sheets, and a catalog of research reports and public education materials.

National Organization for the Reform of Marijuana Laws (NORML)
1001 Connecticut Ave. NW, Suite 710, Washington, DC 20036
(202) 483-5500 • fax: (202) 483-0057
e-mail: norml@norml.org • website: www.norml.org

NORML fights to legalize marijuana and to help those who have been convicted and sentenced for possessing or selling marijuana. In addition to pamphlets and position papers, its website contains a news archive and an online library with links to congressional testimony, research reports, and surveys and polls.

Office of National Drug Control Policy
Drug Policy Information Clearinghouse
PO Box 6000, Rockville, MD 20849-6000
e-mail: ondcp@ncjrs.org • website: www.whitehousedrugpolicy.gov

The Office of National Drug Control Policy is responsible for formulating the government's national drug strategy and the president's antidrug policy as well as coordinating the federal agencies responsible for stopping drug trafficking. Drug policy studies are available upon request.

Partnership for a Drug-Free America
405 Lexington Ave., Suite 1601, New York, NY 10174
(212) 922-1560 • fax: (212) 922-1570
website: www.drugfreeamerica.org

The Partnership for a Drug-Free America is a nonprofit organization that utilizes media communication to reduce demand for illicit drugs in America. Best known for its national antidrug advertising campaign, the partnership works to "unsell" drugs to children and to prevent drug abuse among kids. It publishes the annual *Partnership Newsletter* as well as monthly press releases about current events with which the partnership is involved.

Bibliography

Books

John A. Benson, Stanley J. Watson, and Janet E. Joy, eds.	*Marijuana and Medicine: Assessment of the Science Base.* Washington, DC: National Academy Press, 1999.
Alan Bock	*Waiting to Inhale: The Politics of Medical Marijuana.* Santa Ana, CA: Seven Locks Press, 2000.
Richard J. Bonnie and Charles H. Whitehead II	*Marijuana Conviction: History of Marijuana Prohibition.* New York: Open Society Institute, 1999.
Elizabeth Russell Connelly and Beth Connolly	*Through a Glass Darkly: The Psychological Effects of Marijuana and Hashish.* Broomall, PA: Chelsea, 1998.
Sean Connolly	*Marijuana.* Chicago: Heinemann Library, 2002.
Mitchell Earleywine	*Understanding Marijuana: A New Look at the Scientific Evidence.* New York: Oxford University Press, 2002.
Jennifer James	*All About Marijuana: A Special Report for Young People.* Tempe, AZ: Do It Now Foundation, 1999.
Alison Mack and Janet Joy	*Marijuana as Medicine: The Science Beyond the Controversy.* Washington, DC: National Academy Press, 2000.
Bill McCollum, ed.	*Medical Marijuana Referenda Movement in America.* Washington, DC: DIANE Publishing, 2001.
Brian Preston	*Pot Planet: Adventures in Global Marijuana Culture.* New York: Grove Atlantic, 2002.
Robert C. Randall and Alice M. O'Leary	*Marijuana Rx: The Patients' Fight for Medicinal Pot.* New York: Thunder's Mouth, 1999.
Charles R. Schwenk and Susan L. Rhodes	*Marijuana and the Workplace: Interpreting Research on Complex Social Issues.* Westport, CT: Quorum Books, 1999.
Dan Shapiro	*Mom's Marijuana.* New York: Vintage Books, 2001.
Larry Sloman	*Reefer Madness.* New York: St. Martin's, 1998.
Gary L. Somdahl	*Marijuana Drug Dangers.* Berkeley Heights, NJ: Enslow, 2000.
Debbie Stanley	*Marijuana and Your Lungs: The Incredibly Disgusting Story.* New York: Rosen, 2000.
Robert Thorne	*Marihuana the Burning Bush of Moses: Mysticism and Cannabis Experience.* Portland, OR: Clarus Books, 1999.

Periodicals

Pauline Arrillaga — "Marijuana Growers Ravage U.S. Forests," *Los Angeles Times*, February 26, 2000.

William F. Buckley Jr. — "Who's the Judge of Medical Necessity?" *Los Angeles Times*, May 16, 2001.

Linda Greenhouse — "Justices Set Back Use of Marijuana to Treat Illness," *New York Times*, May 15, 2001.

Lester Grinspoon — "Whither Medical Marijuana?" *Contemporary Drug Problems*, Spring 2000.

Leslie Iverson — "Marijuana: The Myths Are Hazardous to Your Health," *Cerebrum*, Vol. 1, No. 2, 1999.

Hank Kalet — "Reform of Drug Laws Needed," *Progressive Populist*, June 15, 2001.

Sharon Lerner — "Up in Smoke," *Village Voice*, May 22, 2001.

Sara Lyall — "Easing of Marijuana Laws Angers Many Britons," *New York Times*, August 12, 2002.

Peter McWilliams — "A Survivor's Tale," *Liberty*, April 2000.

Mike Mitka — "Therapeutic Marijuana Use Supported While Thorough Proposed Study Done," *JAMA*, April 28, 1999.

Judy Monroe — "Marijuana—A Mind-Altering Drug," *Current Health*, March 1998.

Eileen Moon — "Marijuana As Medicine?" *Professional Counselor*, August 1999.

Eric Schlosser — "The Politics of Pot: A Government in Denial," *Rolling Stone*, March 4, 1999.

Eric Single, Paul Christie, and Robert Ali — "The Impact of Cannabis Decriminalisation in Australia and the United States," *Journal of Public Health Policy*, Vol. 21, No. 2, 2000.

David C. Slade — "Medicinal Marijuana," *World & I*, May 2001.

William E. Stempsey — "The Battle for Medical Marijuana in the War on Drugs," *America*, April 11, 1998.

Stuart Taylor Jr. — "Medical Marijuana and the Folly of the Drug War," *National Journal*, May 19, 2001.

Lynn Zimmer and John Morgan — "Marijuana: Science, Politics and Policy," *Drug Policy Letter*, March/April 2000.

Index